MW00618783

VICTORIA'S
CASTLES

A Brief History of Lovers, Madmen, Millionaires and Ghosts on Canada's Imperial Margins

by

Paul G. Chamberlain

© 2004

Dingle House
Press

Paul G. Chamberlain
Dingle House Press
137 Gorge Road East
Victoria, BC, V9A 1L1

Copyright © 2004 by
Paul G. Chamberlain

Printed and bound in Canada

National Library of Canada Cataloguing in Publication

Chamberlain, Paul Geoffrey, 1953-
Victoria's castles : a brief history of lovers, madmen,
millionaires and ghosts on Canada's imperial margins /
Paul G. Chamberlain.

Includes bibliographical references and index.
ISBN 0-9734317-0-9

1. Castles — British Columbia — Victoria — History.
2. Mansions — British Columbia — Victoria — History.
3. Historic buildings — British Columbia — Victoria.
4. Victoria (B.C.) — History. I. Title.

FC3846.7.C48 2003   971.1'28   C2003-906702-5

Cover: Hatley Park from the north *(AUTHOR)*
Frontispiece: Detail of Government House gate *(AUTHOR)*

Table of Contents

Foreword

*V*ICTORIA'S CASTLES was inspired in part by a series of lectures I gave at the University of Victoria at
the beginning of the new millennium entitled 'Castles: A
Survey of the Spectacle of Power'. As a geographer with
a passion for history, I wanted to explore the castles of
southern Vancouver Island, beginning with an examina-
tion of the genesis of the castle, and ending with a study
of the variety of ways in which castles are represented in
the city's contemporary urban landscape. It became apparent during the course, however, that although much
had been written about local castles, the publications thus
far had tended to focus on specific residences, and I felt
that a compact volume about several local castles might
prove popular. The book begins in medias res, as Homer
would say, so perhaps I should say something at the out-
set about the origin of the castle itself.

The castle was an artifice that emerged at a time when
tribal society was breaking down, and the nation state had
not yet evolved. Originally, therefore, the castle was pri-

marily a defensive site. But it was also the residence of an important person; consequently, it came to be regarded as a symbol of that person's power. Castles evolved throughout Europe in the Middle Ages, but they are also found in other parts of the globe, most notably in Syria, India and Japan. Nevertheless, it was the Normans who had the greatest impact on their design throughout the Western world, and many of the castles discussed in this book owe much to Anglo-Norman traditions.

Castles proliferated in England at an astonishing rate in the aftermath of the Norman Conquest, but they gradually fell into disuse by the beginning of the 14th century because of the advent of gunpowder, the decline of social instability, and a need for greater comfort. By the middle of the 17th century many of England's castles were in ruins, due in no small part to Oliver Cromwell who, fearing a royalist redoubt, reduced many of them to rubble. Curiously, however, the castle enjoyed a renaissance during the 19th century: suddenly, elegant homes sporting a martial facade began to appear all over Britain. The social forces that impelled this curious phenomenon quickly spread across the Atlantic, and this is really where our story begins.

Seven of Vancouver Island's castles are discussed in this book. Unfortunately, only three of them are still standing today; for this reason, our story relies heavily upon archival material. I'd like to thank the British Columbia Archives for allowing me to use their extensive collection of materials; in particular, a special thanks is also extended to the staff at The Craigdarroch Castle Historical Museum Society, the Friends of Hatley Park Society, and the Strata Council of Spencer Castle, who have all been most generous with their time. Once again, I am indebted to Michael Wainwright for his generous assistance in preparing the manuscript for publication. Finally, it is hoped that in writing this volume more people will be encouraged to visit these fine homes, and contribute to their legacy.

Paul G. Chamberlain
Victoria, 2004

Introduction

IT IS CURIOUS that a city so far from England is blessed with so many elegant castles. In the heart of Victoria stands Craigdarroch Castle, built by a coal baron to fulfil a promise to his sweetheart; nearby is Spencer Castle, once the home of a family of retail magnates, whose business eventually became part of the famed T. Eaton Company; and not far away is Hatley Castle, its halls haunted still by the ghost of a young lady, pining for her lost lover. Several more castles once graced Canada's imperial margins, but they have long since vanished from Victoria's skyline, victims of neglect, fire and the wrecking ball. This is their story.

Why were so many castles built in Victoria? Part of the reason is money. Investment first began to trickle into the city when the Hudson's Bay Company established a fur trading post at Fort Victoria in 1843. Recognising the strategic importance of the site, the Royal Navy quickly set up a naval base, further bolstering the city's economy; but in 1858 an event occurred which was to have a dramatic impact upon the city — it was gripped by gold fever. By the end of the Cariboo gold rush, Victoria was not only more wealthy, but it had firmly established itself as the capital of the Colony of Vancouver Island, a role that would later expand to include the entire territory of British Columbia. Fur brought men to this fine city; however, it was gold, lumber, coal, agriculture, fishing, real estate and retailing that inflated the pockets of the city's richest businessmen, and this made it inevitable that conspicuous consumption would be reflected in their grand residences — but why castles?

An important clue lies in the ethnic composition of the city. Victoria's financial elite in those days were almost all British; many were of Scottish extraction, a good number having come to British Columbia to work for the Hudson's Bay Company. So, what better way was there for a millionaire to stamp his imprimatur on the city than to replicate the Old World in the New by drawing upon the iconography of the landed aristocracy in the form of a castle? But money and family ties to the Old Country are only part of the explanation for this curious phenomenon.

An architectural movement known as Romantic Gothic Revivalism was sweeping across Canada during the 19th century. It was driven in part by the Camden Society, a rather obscure 19th century Anglican organisation based in Cambridge that extolled the 'High Gothic' with its pointed windows, its crenellated roofs and its lofty towers. For almost fifty years nearly all Anglican churches in Canada were built according to its precepts, and the Camden Society's attempt to replicate the noble spirit of medieval architecture throughout the British Empire was further bolstered by the Victorian art critic John Ruskin, who felt that Gothic architecture was ideally suited to an age of social reform; others, such as William Morris, simply saw it as an apposite instrument to help mitigate the harmful effects of the Industrial Revolution by fostering a sense of nostalgia for the past.

Implicit within this nostalgia for the past was a romantic twist. Gothic Revivalism was propelled in part by new tastes in art, a growing interest in archaeology, and a fondness for gothic literature; it was no accident, therefore, that the proliferation of castles in the English countryside was soon replicated in Canada. Perhaps the most well known castle in Canada is Casa Loma. Built at the turn of the last century in Toronto by an eccentric millionaire named Sir Henry Pellat, this gigantic edifice boasts a labyrinth of high corbelled turrets, imposing battlements, Tudor chimneys and pointed windows. In addition to Casa Loma, other notable castles also made their appearance in Ontario, including Holland House, Birkett Castle, Ainsley House, and Castle Hamilton. Ostentatiously embellished with towers, battlements and pointed windows, their iconography reflected a thirst for the Gothic, as well as the wealth of their residents, who yearned to replicate English tastes. They were ideas that were beginning to make their presence felt on Canada's imperial margins.

Cary Castle

IN ITS EARLY DAYS Victoria looked very different than it does today. In the words of one journalist: "It was a remarkable place, [with] wooden shanties here, there and everywhere... many of them not much more than lean-tos, [each] built at odd angles and on odd corners." One fine morning George Hunter Cary changed all that. A somewhat eccentric character, Cary had just survived a harrowing journey around Cape Horn on a windjammer when he marched into Victoria with a pile of law books under his arm to become the Colony's first Attorney General. Not content to merely administer the law, however, Cary bought a gold mine in the Cariboo and, eagerly anticipating a lucky strike, he banged on the door of a local engineer named Fred Walter Green, demanding that he build him a castle.

Cary chose a remote windy site on top of Rockland Avenue overlooking the Straits of Juan de Fuca. Unfortunately, his gold mine proved less profitable than he expected, and he was forced to scale back his plans considerably. Cary Castle was built in 1860: it boasted a three-storey drum-tower, with a porte-cochère at one end (not unlike a barbican), and an enormous bay window at the other; the roof was festooned with battlements, supported by corbels. One historian later described it as "vaguely reminiscent of a semi-ruined Scottish border castle;" but another was less flattering, calling it "a queer architectural intrusion on the land-

Cary Castle as it looked in the early 1860s
BCA: A-01660

scape [that was] eccentric to the point of madness."

No sooner had Cary Castle been built, however, than some began to wonder if the Attorney General himself wasn't a little mad. On more than one occasion he was stopped for galloping his horse across the Bay Street Bridge, terrifying local residents; several of his legal decisions were equally embarrassing over the years. Judge Begbie — himself a rather colourful character — noted that "genius and madness in him were closely combined;" and it was only a matter of time

Architect John Wright
BCA: A-02546

before Cary's career came crashing to a halt. Eventually, Sir James Douglas dismissed him, sending the disgraced Attorney General back to England where he subsequently went insane.

George Hunter Cary might have been mad, but he wasn't stupid: in 1865 Cary Castle was sold for 19 000 dollar. However, before it became the official residence for the new Governor some modifications were required. The man chosen to make these alterations was John Wright, an architect who had set up the first profes-

Cary Castle after the alterations, circa 1868
BCA: A-02820

sional practice in the city in 1859. Wright was born in Scotland, and by all accounts had a profound influence on the city, one historian going as far as to assert that he "changed the architectural thinking of Victoria." In 1866 the renovations were complete, and were considered by everybody to be a credit to the exemplary skill of the Scottish architect. Although the three-storey tower was retained, the porte-cochère was bricked up, the bay windows were expanded, and a dormered roof was added to the French Norman Hall. Merlons and embrasures, supported by decorative corbels, embellished the roof line, and tall Tudor chimneys were superimposed on top of the new residence, lending an air of regal sobriety to its martial facade.

Arthur Kennedy was the first Governor privileged to reside at Cary Castle, but in the next few years he was succeeded by a list of dignitaries, all of whom were subjected to a remarkable degree of public scrutiny. Clement Francis Cornwall, for example, was born in England: a Cambridge man, he had a passion for cricket, a love of horses and a keen interest in ranching. Lieutenant Governor Cornwall had been elected to the Provincial Legislature in 1862, and became a senator a decade later. Finally, he was appointed Lieutenant Governor of the Province in 1881. Cary Castle was a bright and happy place in Governor Cornwall's era — two children were born to his wife, Charlotte, during their residence. Unfortunately, the lack of formal dinners led some to question seriously a renewal of his tenure, prompting one local journalist to note: "It is scarcely necessary to say that the reappointment of Mr. Cornwall would not be popular." The public was not disappointed. Governor Cornwall soon retired in Victoria, but he lived well into the next century, dying at the age of 74. His eldest daughter was not so fortunate — she died of a rattlesnake bite.

Lieutenant Governor Hugh Nelson was a more popular man, however. Born in Ireland, his career followed a similar path to his predecessor, amassing a small fortune in the lumber business, before entering politics. After holding a seat in the Provincial Legislature for several years, Nelson was then elected to the

The Honourable Lieutenant Governor Hugh Nelson
BCA: A-01848

House of Commons in Ottawa; and, like Cornwall, he subsequently became a senator. Hugh Nelson capped off his illustrious career by being appointed British Columbia's fourth Lieutenant Governor in 1887. A contemporary journalist optimistically predicted: "We may confidently look for much of the old-time geniality which was always characteristic of the gubernatorial (sic) residence." Evidently the *Colonist* was delighted, and at Nelson's inaugural ball, later that year, the newspaper was pleased to report "how well the Governor appeared and with what naturalness the position of representative of the Queen seemed to become him." Lavish festivities continued throughout his administration. At a summer garden party in 1890, for example, over 300 guests were in attendance, savouring sumptuous delicacies on tables glistening with silverware, while they listened to the melodious sound of the band of H.M.S. Warspite playing in the garden. There was a general agreement that Governor Nelson proved "a genial and [a] wise administrator."

Yet Cary Castle evoked some rather ambivalent sentiments over the years. On a state visit in 1876, Lady Dufferin was shocked to walk downstairs one morning to discover six prisoners polishing the ballroom floor with chains on their ankles; however, on another visit, Princess Louise was charmed by the castle, describing it as "halfway between heaven and Balmoral." Hyperbole aside, Cary Castle was cold, windy and damp, and one journalist noted how "the wind whistle[d] through the numerous cracks and crevices in the walls; the roof leak[ed] in spite of constant patching; [and] cold draughts penetrate[d] all parts." Cary Castle, it seems, was Victoria's first leaky condo. However, there was an even more serious hazard lurking in the wings — fire. Smoke billowed from the castle on several occasions, and only the timely application of a bucket of

water managed to douse the flames. But in 1899 a conflagration erupted that was to prove disastrous.

Cary Castle in ruins after the disastrous fire of 1899
BCA: G-02606

It occurred during the appointment of Lieutenant
Governor Thomas Robert McInnes. Governor McInnes
was a dour Scot who had an aversion to alcohol. Per-

haps it was just as well he cultivated sobriety, because when he came down to breakfast that fateful morning it was not the sound of bacon and eggs he heard crackling in the frying pan, but burning rafters. McInnes had just enough time to rush upstairs, and throw his ceremonial uniform out of the window, before he was forced to run the gauntlet of falling timbers in a desperate attempt to save his life. The castle was not so fortunate; sadly, Cary Castle burnt to the ground. Had George Hunter Cary put a curse on the castle, people wondered? We will never know, but as the residents of Victoria gazed in horror at the ruins that morning, George Hunter Cary's spirit must have been lingering in the ashes. Later, the Province commented pitifully: "This picturesque old pile, of all and no styles of architecture, was one of the most historic as well as one of the oldest residential buildings of British Columbia." It was to be several years before Cary Castle rose from the ashes, but by then other castles had appeared in Victoria — one of them was Armadale Castle.

DIRECTIONS: Cary Castle once stood on the grounds of today's Government House. From Downtown go north on Government Street; turn right on to Fort street; turn right on Cook Street; then make an immediate left turn on to Rockland Avenue. Gardens are open from sunrise to sunset. It is a 45 minute walk from the Inner Harbour.

Armadale

THE STORY OF ARMADALE CASTLE begins on a Spring morning in 1851, when a young man stands on the deck of a sailing ship, and catches his first glimpse of Vancouver Island low on the horizon. His name is William John Macdonald. Like Cary, he sailed around the Horn, suffered from seasickness, and was forced to survive for months on sea rations, later noting in his diary: "[O]ur food by this time, three weeks out, became bad and scarce, cheese and biscuits full of weevils, water scarce and putrid part of the time." Macdonald must have felt relieved when he was finally rowed ashore in a war canoe manned by Native Indians.

Unlike George Hunter Cary, Macdonald was a Scotsman. After surviving a potato famine on the Isle of Skye, he had sailed to Victoria at the age 19 to start a new life as a custom's collector for the Hudson's Bay Company. When his mother waved goodbye to her son, she must have wondered if she would ever see him again. Although Macdonald did not lack initiative—

he had served as the private secretary to Admiral Fishbourne-Portree during the potato blight in Scotland — it was obvious that he was not destined to remain in the employ of the Hudson's Bay Company for long. In 1858 he left the company to start his own business, 'Reid and Macdonald'; and, like so many businessmen of that era, he took full advantage of the opportunities afforded to him during the Cariboo gold rush. Investing heavily in

William John Macdonald,
circa 1860
BCA: A-01500

property, Macdonald soon became a wealthy man. He was subsequently elected to the Provincial Legislature, and, in 1866, became mayor of the city; Macdonald crowned his career with an appointment to the Senate in Ottawa. By this time his thoughts had turned to building a castle.

For many years the Macdonalds lived at Glendale Cottage, but runaway horses, the dust from nearby factories, and his large family — three sons and three daughters — made a move inevitable. But why did Macdonald decide to build a castle? It's possible that he was inspired by Cary Castle, the 'gubernatorial' residence on top of the hill; however, the Senator's wealth, his British heritage, and the growing popularity of Gothic Revivalism would also have influenced his decision. But unlike Cary Castle, which was built overlooking the city on Rockland Avenue on a site reminiscent of a motte, Macdonald selected a less imposing location for his residence in James Bay. The only task left was to find an architect. If John Wright had still been living in Victoria, his task might have been a little easier, but Wright closed his architectural practice in the city in 1867 and moved to San Francisco; so, Macdonald hired the services of another local architect instead — a builder who "did plans." His name was Thomas Trounce. But rather than christen his castle with an eponymous title, as Cary had done, Macdonald chose to name his residence 'Armadale' after his ancestral home on the Isle of Skye. His mother would have been proud.

A more apt description of Armadale, however, might be a villa residence with a martial face. It was certainly a less imposing residence than Cary Castle. Essentially a gabled residence, the castle was flanked on one side by a square turret, and on the other by a more modest wing that helped to give the impression of a cross-axial floor plan. With the skilful assistance of a W.H. Courtnay, a stonemason, Trounce embellished the roof line with crenellations, and adorned the turret with imitation loops, which accentuated its martial facade. The interior was equally impressive.

Inside the main entrance was a long hallway leading into a spacious drawing room with a 13-foot high

Architect Thomas Trounce
BCA: 4406

ceiling. Next door was a dinning room, which looked out onto a veranda, and nearby was an adjoining library with a bay window. The kitchen was generously equipped with an array of modern appliances, and a staircase led upstairs to the bedrooms. Outside was a store room, a dairy and a coal shed. Armadale sat on a 28-acre estate that resembled a medieval bailey: within its confines were natural woodlands, a fine garden, and a bridal path for romantic walks on a summer's afternoon. For more energetic guests, there was a tennis court.

In its day Armadale was one of the finest homes

Armadale Castle
BCA: 06687

in Victoria, and Mrs. Macdonald wasted no time in introducing it to the public. In November, 1877, a soirée was held at the castle, and the memorable occasion was documented by a local journalist: "The spacious mansion was thrown open to guests, " he wrote, and "[t]wo of the largest rooms were devoted to dancing, which was maintained until an early hour in the morning."

Other celebrations followed. In 1890, for example, Senator Macdonald's eldest daughter, Flora, was married to Mr. Hamilton, the manager of the Bank of British North America. Another wedding was celebrated at

Macdonald family portrait
(Senator Macdonald seated at right; Mrs. Macdonald seated second from left)
BCA: B-00084

Armadale in 1896, when the second of their three daughters was married to a naval officer. After the service, the happy couple was escorted to the castle in style: "Not content with hauling their commander and his bride direct to Armadale, the jacktars, with great enthusiasm, took the carriage round Douglas, Yates and Government Streets, across the bridge and so to Senator Macdonald's beautiful residence, where the sailors were given a lunch." By this time they must have worked up quite an appetite.

Senator Macdonald spent many of his later years in Ottawa, but he never lost touch with his Scottish roots. All of his sons were educated in Scotland, and on one poignant occasion he returned to his birthplace on the Isle of Skye to visit his mother, who was overjoyed to see her son again after such a long absence. It was during one such holiday that the Beeton's came to stay at Armadale.

Henry Coppinger Beeton was a close friend of Senator Macdonald. In the 1870s he had founded a wholesale business with several partners; it was called

Henry Coppinger Beeton, circa 1870
BCA: A-01992

'Turner, Beeton and Tunstall'. Later, he served as Agent General for British Columbia in London, where he "talked up British Columbia" with great enthusiasm. One of Beeton's sons served in the Imperial Forces, fight ing in the Boxer Rebellion in China; on his return from Manchuria he donated an enormous iron bell to the city, which sat in Beacon Hill Park for many years. Another son, Cecil, went on to distinguish himself as a celebrated royal photographer. Sadly, a third son died prematurely in Victoria in 1882; Senator Macdonald was a pall bearer at the funeral, and his father later donated a stained glass window to St. John's Church in his son's memory. The Beeton's spent many happy years in Victoria and, after Mr. Beeton finally retired to England, he named his home in Weston-Super-Mare 'Armadale' in memory of his happy years spent in Canada.

In 1913 Senator Macdonald's wife fell gravely ill. Suffering great pain, he noted sadly how "a merciful God [finally] called her to her long home, leaving her children and myself in great sorrow." By this time Macdonald himself was feeling his age, and he sold his castle, taking up residence in a more modest home in Oak Bay, where he died at the age of 84. He received a glowing obituary in the *Colonist*, which described at some length how "[h]e never lost interest, as so many did with advancing years, in the welfare of the city where so many of his years were spent."

Armadale Castle continued to grace Victoria's skyline for many more years, but it never regained its former glory. As the years went by its facade slowly began to crumble: first it was turned into an apartment complex; then it suffered the indignity of being used as a nightclub; finally, it became an officer's mess for the Royal Canadian Navy. In 1944 it fell victim to the wrecking ball. Macdonald Park now occupies the site of Armadale Castle, and all traces of the residence have long gone. However, Trounce Alley in downtown Victoria is named in honour of the man who built the house. As for the bell, well, that sits quietly in the Victoria Art Gallery on Moss Street — few are aware of its existence today, let alone its connection to Armadale Castle.

DIRECTIONS: Armadale Castle once stood on the grounds of today's Macdonald Park in James Bay. From downtown go south on Government Street; turn right on Belleville Street; and then turn left on Oswego Street. It is a 15 minute walk from the Inner Harbour.

Craigdarroch Castle

ACCORDING TO A POPULAR LEGEND, Robert Dunsmuir promised to build his wife a castle if she would leave Scotland and settle with him in Canada. Evidently she agreed, and the result was a stunning castle that has become a permanent fixture in the city's landscape. Craigdarroch Castle was designed on a hitherto unimaginable scale; its soaring turrets are indeed reminiscent of the home of a Scottish laird, and the man who built it might just as easily have stepped out of a novel by Sir Walter Scott. But Robert Dunsmuir was no fictional character. By combining hard work, luck, and a shrewd sense for making money, he managed to found a family dynasty that shaped the city's destiny for several generations.

Robert Dunsmuir sailed from London Docks in 1850. His companions included his young wife, Joan; their two eldest children, Elizabeth and Agnes; and Robert Dunsmuir's uncle, Boyd Gilmore. But it was far from a relaxing journey: near the end of their voyage the 'Pekin' ran aground in the Columbia River, and the crew promptly abandoned ship to seek their fortune in the California gold fields. By now Joan was probably having second thoughts about the whole venture; fortunately, the Dunsmuir family quickly secured a berth on the 'Mary Dare', which took them the remain-

Robert Dunsmuir
BCA: A-01253

der of the journey up the coast of Vancouver Island to Fort Rupert, where Robert Dunsmuir began work as the manager of a coal mine for the Hudson's Bay Company.

Robert Dunsmuir was born near Kilmarnock in Ayrshire, the scion of a family of mine mangers who had worked relentlessly for wealthy landowners for generations. Dunsmuir might have suffered a similar fate labouring for the Hudson's Bay Company in British Columbia had it not been for a stroke of good fortune. One night in 1869, after a fortuitous move from Fort Rupert to Nanaimo, legend has it that Dunsmuir was stumbling home intoxicated when he accidentally discovered a coal seam under an uprooted tree — black gold! The canny Scot quickly staked a claim, sought financial backing from several partners in the Royal Navy, and then signed a contract to supply Her Majesty's ships with coal. Resigning from the Hudson's Bay Company, Dunsmuir never looked back. In an age of steam, coal was king, and in less than a generation Dunsmuir was crowned the richest man in western Canada.

Not content to limit himself solely to a local market, however, in 1875 the crafty Scot began exporting his black gold to San Francisco; to facilitate this ambitious endeavour, he acquired a fleet of steamships powered by — you guessed it — coal. Dunsmuir subsequently added the Albion Iron Works and the Daily British Colonist to his financial empire, capping his career with a seat in the Provincial Legislature in 1882. When the Province wanted a railway built from Nanaimo to Victoria, Dunsmuir agreed to lay the 75 miles of track, in exchange for 750 000 dollars, nearly two million acres of land, and, of course, more mineral rights. When the first iron horse finally pulled into Victoria on the Esquimalt and Nanaimo Railway in 1888, Dunsmuir was given a hero's welcome. Unfortunately, not everybody cheered: the founder of the Dunsmuir Dynasty had made some bitter enemies in his short, but astonishing, career.

In the 19th century coal mining was a very dangerous business. Not surprisingly, Dunsmuir's mines were plagued by accidents. In 1888, for example, a terrifying explosion in one colliery killed 77 miners. Tragic as this was, Robert Dunsmuir's first reaction to such news was often: "Have any horses been injured?" Given the difficult working conditions, and the relatively low pay, it was inevitable that Dunsmuir would have labour strife. One of the most serious incidents occurred after Dunsmuir had demanded that his miners take a pay cut due to a slump in coal prices; but later, when suspicions were voiced that the clever Scot was tampering with the weigh scales — short changing the miners' wages still further — serious trouble erupted. Things got so bad by 1877 that the militia had to be despatched from Victoria to restore order. What was Dunsmuir's long term solution? Simple: hire more Chinese labour. Of the 77 men killed in the explosion in 1888, 46 were Chinese. But Dunsmuir's unpopularity wasn't confined to his labour practices. Indiscreet comments that the future of the Province would be best served by annexation with the United States did not go unnoticed in London, and probably cost him a knighthood.

Robert Dunsmuir never did get a title, but he did become rich. In less than a generation the coal baron transformed a five-dollar-a-week job as a mine manger into a financial empire conservatively estimated at 15 million dollars, making him one of the wealthiest men in Canada. By this time the Dunsmuirs were living in Victoria at a residence called 'Fairview'. Now approaching retirement, and with several of the family's ten children still living at home, Robert Dunsmuir's thoughts inevitably turned to something more ambitious. It was time to fulfil a promise to his wife — Craigdarroch Castle was about to be born.

By 1888 Robert Dunsmuir had acquired 28 acres of property overlooking the city not far from Cary Castle. But unlike Cary Castle and Armadale Castle, each of which exhibit strong Anglo-Norman features, Craigdarroch was to be a radical departure in style; it has often been called a Scottish baronial castle, and it is easy to see why when you catch your first glimpse of its pointed turrets. Moreover, like Armadale, it's name harkens back to Dunsmuir's ancestral homeland: 'Craigdarroch' means 'rocky oak place' in Gaelic. However, a closer inspection of Craigdarroch Castle reveals a more complex pedigree. Superimposed on the Scottish facade is both a chateauesque roof line, and an Italianate veranda. A clue to help unravel this mystery lies in the architect who built it.

In the years that led up to the construction of Craigdarroch Castle, Robert Dunsmuir made several visits to San Francisco. It is possible that on one of these visits Dunsmuir spoke with John Wright, the architect who had once worked on Cary Castle, and who was now living in California. In the end, however, the coal baron selected an architect from Oregon to build his castle: his name was Warren Heyward Williams. No record of the communication between Robert Dunsmuir and Warren Heyward Williams has survived; but Williams was already well known in Victoria. In 1886 he built the Bank of British Columbia, which still stands to this day at the corner of Government and Fort Street, and which one local journalist of the period praised as the "most perfect piece of architecture so far existing in this Province." In addition, Williams may also have built an extension onto 'Fairview', suggesting that he was already well known to the Dunsmuirs. Although it will never be known precisely what the two men discusssed, their conversation would certainly have included some reference to the castles being built in San Francisco at that time.

Perhaps the most famous castle in San Francisco in the 1880s was the home constructed for Mark Hopkins, a railway baron who once lived on Nob Hill. With a fortune at his disposal, Hopkins had commissioned the services of John Wright, who built the 'bonanza king' a residence with stylistic features very similar to those that would later appear in Craigdarroch Castle. Although the parallel is too much to be mere coincidence, it would be unfair to accuse Warren Heyward Williams of imitating John Wright's work: Williams undertook his own apprenticeship in San Francisco with his father, Stephen Hiddon Williams, and the son was well known for his Italian Renaissance style, which he combined with a Victorian Picturesque tradition.

Nevertheless, it is of interest to note that there is a photograph in the archives at Craigdarroch Castle of a gatehouse at a large estate on America's East Coast that bares an uncanny resemblance to Craigdarroch Castle. Was Williams familiar with this building, and did he show it to Robert Dunsmuir during their conversations? Possibly — but in the end we should not underestimate Robert Dunsmuir's desire to replicate his Scottish heritage in the design of his castle. The name 'Craigdarroch' was probably his idea, although it is interesting to note that a stately home by this name already existed in Scotland, making it hardly original.

By 1887 the plans for Craigdarroch Castle were complete. However, in contrast to the city's two Anglo-Norman castles, which were partly constructed on a cross-axial floor plan, Craigdarroch was designed with a more compact, perpendicular profile in mind. Specifically, instead of incorporating a crenellated keep, which had been used in each of Victoria's earlier castles, Craigdarroch was to be dominated by a tall, cylindrical turret with a conical roof, lending the building its Scottish baronial appearance. A less ostentatious turret was attached to the south side of the building. But the remainder of Craigdarroch Castle exhibits a polyglot of styles, rendering it highly eclectic in design, and Warren Heyward Williams' signature is clearly evident here. A closer look at the building supports this conclusion.

On the north side of the castle, for example, is a porte-cochère, which frames the main entrance to the building. On the west side is another entrance next to a loggia, or covered Italianate veranda, which extends along the south side of the castle, where the porch can be accessed by yet another flight of stone steps. As the eye is drawn upwards small windows can be seen, some protruding outwards as oriels with Victorian balconies; others are set in Romanesque archways, and still others are capped with pointed, gothic brickwork, adding variety to the symmetry of the roof line, which terminates in finials. Here, tall Tudor chimneys rise majestically above the French Loire roof, the latter fretted with red tiles. Finally, rought ironwork decorates the building, and includes a chemin de ronde, a walkway that surrounds the upper part of the enormous turret that crowns the castle's north side.

Porte-cochère at the entrance to Craigdarroch Castle
AUTHOR

It is estimated that Craigdarroch cost 500 000 dollars to build — an enormous sum in its day — but much of it was spent on decorating the interior. Due to its perpendicular profile, Craigdarroch Castle is remarkably compact: it comprises 39 rooms, which are built on four levels — five if you include the cellar. Entering the main entrance on the north side, the visitor is greeted by the Grand Hall. A fireplace set in white oak panelling dominates the entrance, evoking a baronial residence in the Highlands of Scotland. Adjoining the hall on the main floor are a drawing room, a dining room, and a library, the latter for gentlemen to enjoy a postprandial cigar amid the Spanish Mahogany decor. Stained glass windows, ornate mantelpieces, and florid quotations from Shakespeare adorn the rooms downstairs. A staircase leads upstairs to Mrs. Dunsmuir's sitting room, the bedrooms, a billiard room, a modest dance hall, and, finally, a small room at the top of the tower.

View of Craigdarroch from the southwest clearly displaying the loggia
AUTHOR

In contrast to the exterior massing of the building, however, one is struck by the compactness of the rooms inside the castle; it is a feeling accentuated even more by the paucity of light entering the tiny windows. One is given the impression that although the castle was built overlooking the city to be seen by everybody from outside, what went on inside the castle was intensely

View of Caigdarroch from the west showing the Victorian balconies
AUTHOR

private. An enormous garden, which resembled a medieval ward, once mediated between this private world within the castle, and the public space beyond. Sadly, this has almost completely disappeared. Today, the visitor must imagine the terraced gardens, the bountiful orchards and the magnificent groves of oak trees that once adorned the property. In the early days a lodge guarded the long curving driveway that led up to the main entrance, but this too has now vanished.

In its day Craigdarroch Castle was by far the most

lavish home ever built in Victoria. But Warren Heyward Williams could not have undertaken such an ambitious project without a revolution in North America's transportation system. Although the stone was quarried locally, the stained glass windows, the bright red tiles on the roof, and the wood panelling were all imported, the latter courtesy of A.H. Andrews and Company of Boston. For this reason, some experts characterise Craigdarroch as a 'mail order castle' — a rather pejorative term, but a reminder that unlike Victoria's earlier castles this residence was a harbinger of what would later become the modern consumer society. Specifically,

View of Caigdarroch from the northwest with the chemin de ronde
visible at the upper left
AUTHOR

what made Craigdarroch different from Cary Castle and Armadale Castle was not just its cost, but the geographical diversity of its building materials, something that would have been impossible without the advent of the railway. It was a revolution in transportation technology with which Robert Dunsmuir was very familiar.

Craigdarroch was built in less than two years, but the project was not without some challenging complications. Barely four months into the construction of the castle, Warren Heyward Williams suddenly died, leaving his draftsman, Arthur Smith, in charge of the project. In 1889 Robert Dunsmuir himself fell ill, succumbing to a cold, which soon developed into a serious infection that eventually took his life. With the castle still unfinished, Dunsmuir lay in state in his old home of Fairview and, with an unusually florid degree of sentimentality, the *Colonist* reported how "[t]he genial, kindly face, the finely chiseled lips and the square determined chin, every feature so well known and so long to be remembered, was perfect in its repose." Of course, not everybody was sad to see Dunsmuir go, but many Victorians keenly felt his loss, sensing the end of an era with his passing. Craigdarroch Castle was no longer just a symbol of the power that he once exercised over British Columbia, it was now a monument to his life.

First, however, the castle had to be finished. This was a responsibility that now fell upon the shoulders of Mrs. Dunsmuir. Joan's instructions were simple: "Do it as cheaply as possible," she told the landscaper, Hugh Campbell, "but do it right." Arthur Smith must have been a little nonplussed. Joan was now one of the richest women in the North America — why was she being so frugal? Perhaps Joan was alarmed at the escalating cost of the project; or, perhaps she simply had other priorities. Inevitably, there was a decline in the quality of construction towards the end: to this day, for example, there are still no steps leading up to a door on the north side of the building beside the turret. Presumably this was not an oversight, but one of the last minute cost-cutting measures adopted by Arthur Smith, as he

Joan Dunsmuir
BCA: A-01256

put the finishing touches to the building. Nevertheless, satisfied that the castle was now in capable hands, Joan went on holiday with her family to Europe. It was a big family.

Joan Dunsmuir was left with a family of two sons,

and eight daughters. Her eldest son, James, managed the company's sprawling interests in British Columbia, while her younger son, Alex, supervised the office in San Francisco. Joan's main priority, however, was marrying off her eight daughters. After returning from Europe in 1890 to take up residence in Craigdarroch Castle, she began to search assiduously for eligible candidates. The dowager was particularly adept at ferreting out penniless aristocrats — gentlemen with titles but no money. Joan hit pay dirt in 1891 when she married Jessie to Sir Richard John Musgrave, an indigent Irish knight; in 1898, another daughter, Henrietta Maude,

Jessie and bridesmaids outside Craigdarroch Castle on the occasion of her wedding to Sir Richard John Musgrave in 1891
BCA: D-03604

was married to Lieutenant Reginald Spencer Chaplin; and in 1901 Joan arranged the marriage of Annie

Euphemia to Somerset Arthur Gough-Calthorpe, earning the couple an entry in *Debrett's Peerage*. Unfortunately, much of 'Effie's' long life was spent in lunatic asylums. Given the family problems which erupted after Robert Dunsmuir's death, this was hardly surprising.

A squabble broke out almost as soon as James Dunsmuir had been put to rest in the family plot. "Take what you want," the thrifty Scot used to tell his sons, "just don't want too much." Although James and Alex both served their father faithfully over the years, each labouring under the pretext that one day they would both inherit the family business, the shrewd Scot had a surprise for them when he died: Joan was named the principle beneficiary in Robert's will — not the two sons. Instead, James and Alex were to manage the company for their mother. Joan found herself in an enviable position, and these must have seemed like the best years of her life. Legend has it that each morning she would climb the 87 steps to the top of the turret overlooking the city, where she would read the gossip in the morning newspaper, oversee the family business, and plan her daughters' weddings. However, when Joan began spending the family fortune on lavish bridal gifts for her daughters, both the sons felt that unless they wrestled control of the business from their mother, she would soon squander the entire fortune until there was nothing left. A long legal battle ensued.

Alex had managed the company's San Francisco operation for several years, and both brothers felt it prudent to pry this branch of the business out of their mother's hands first. However, this acrimonious situation was not resolved until 1896, nearly a decade after Robert Dunsmuir's death, when it was finally agreed that Joan should give control of the San Francisco operation to Alex. But the brothers were not finished. It took another two years for James to persuade his mother to sign over to him the ownership of all the coal mines on Vancouver Island as well. It seemed as if the family fortune was finally secure. Unfortunately, Alex died suddenly in New York in 1900, triggering yet another battle. Ostensibly, it had been agreed that in the event of the death of Alex his shares would revert back to Joan; when she discovered that Alex had changed his will at the last minute, leaving all his shares to James, who was now the Premier of the Province of British Columbia, Joan fired back. In 1901 her lawsuit made the front page of the *New York Times* — 'Premier of BC sued by his own mother!'

James Dunsmuir now found himself in the rather unenviable position of fighting not just his mother, but his sisters as well. It was a situation not unlike that of his late brother. In many ways Alex was a rather tragic figure. He had fallen in love with his 'landlady', Josephine Wallace, while working in the Unites States. For years, however, his parents had refused to entertain the prospect of their son marrying a divorced woman, but as soon as Alex had safely wrestled control of the business from his mother, he married Josephine anyway. Unfortunately, Alex's happiness was not to last: his untimely death in New York as the new century dawned only confirmed what many had already suspected — years of unhappiness had led him to seek refuge in alcohol.

Lurid details of Alex's scandalous behaviour soon surfaced at the trial. Joan's lawyers attempted to show that Alex was not competent to change his will. Witnesses were paraded before the court to testify how Alex would bribe bartenders to keep saloons open after closing time; how he threw money out of the upstairs window of his hotel room to people on the street below; and how on one occasion he thought he actually saw fish swimming around his bed, and ordered the bellhop not to come too close in case he frightened them away! To complicate matters still further, his new bride, Josephine, died of cancer in the middle of the lengthy trial, and her daughter, a popular New York actress named Edna Wallace Hopper, launched her own lawsuit against James Dunsmuir for Alex's estate.

The legal wrangling lasted until 1906. In their final ruling the court upheld the change to Alex's will, arguing that although he had personal failings he was, nevertheless, a sound businessman. As a result, James Dunsmuir now had complete control of the company's sprawling interests from Vancouver Island to San Francisco; Edna, it was decided, should only inherit San Leandro — her parent's home in Oakland, California. Joan, however, got virtually nothing at all for her efforts. Climbing the 87 steps to the top of her turret at Craigdarroch Castle, she must have felt bitterly disappointed as she gazed out sadly over the city that had once greeted her husband as a hero. When James came to Craigdarroch, cap in hand, to offer to pay his mother's legal expenses, she refused to see him; legend has it that Joan never spoke to her son again.

At her funeral in 1908 Joan's daughter's must have

glared angrily at James, as he sobbed quietly at the back of the church. Yet in typical Dunsmuir fashion, Joan seemed to transcend the family's difficulties in death; one historian summed up Joan Dunsmuir's life with these kind words: "She was a woman of strong character and vigorous mind, a wide reader, keenly interested in politics and in public events." No one, however, could ignore her bitter disappointment at losing control of the Dunsmuir Dynasty — especially her daughters, who were about to experience a humiliation of their own.

In 1909, the castle historian Sydney Jackman would one day describe as "Balmoral blown across the Atlantic," was put up for sale. Although Joan's five surviving daughters inherited Craigdarroch, they could not afford to keep it. Craigdarroch Castle was on the chopping block: the contents were unceremoniously auctioned off, and the castle was quickly bought by a shrewd chartered accountant named Griffith R. Hughes, who promptly subdivided the 28 acres of land into 144 lots. Unable to sell the lots, however, due to a collapse in the local real estate market, Hughes devised a lottery instead — 99 purchasers eventually acquiring 120 lots at 2 750 dollars each. Craigdarroch Castle was sold separately to Solomon Cameron; unfortunately, it turned out to be rather a bad investment. Cameron later failed to pay his property taxes, and when it was clear he couldn't afford the 300 000 dollars he owed the creditors, the Bank of Montreal foreclosed on the property.

Never again would Craigdarroch Castle be used as a private residence. In 1919 it was taken over by the Federal Government, who used the facility as a military hospital. In a little over 18 months it was turned into Victoria College; among its many students was the Canadian journalist Pierre Berton, who demonstrated that the pen was mightier than the cue by carving his name in the billiard room upstairs. Unfortunately, the college became very cramped for space, and in 1946 it was relocated; that year Craigdarroch was converted into an office for the local School Board. But the castle

View of Craigdarroch from the south
AUTHOR

reinvented itself yet again in 1969, when it became the home of the Victoria Conservatory of Music; finally, in 1979, it was decided to move the music school, and after heated debate Craigdarroch Castle was finally converted into a museum. In recent years its staff have worked diligently to return Craigdarroch Castle to its former glory.

Today the castle still looks much as it did in the time of the Dunsmuirs. Unfortunately, the interior has undergone significant alterations over the years, and virtually none of the furnishings inside are original; moreover, as already noted, Craigdarroch no longer occupies the spacious gardens that it once did — nowadays it is encroached on all sides by a residential neighborhood that basks in the shadow of the castle's elegant silhouette. Yet despite this transformation, Craigdarroch still dominates the city from its lofty vantage point at the top of Joan Crescent, attracting hundreds of thousands of visitors each year to savour its history. It even lifts its drawbridge occasionally to wedding receptions, and film crews have fallen in love with the place, bringing in stars like Phyllis Diller and James Garner, much to the delight of viewers around the world. More recently, Craigdarroch was featured on the popular television series 'America's Castles'.

Of all the castles built in Victoria, Craigdarroch seems to strike the most romantic chord in the viewer. Part of the reason, perhaps, is that it is such a clear departure from the traditional Anglo-Norman design exhibited by Cary and Armadale. It is as if Craigdarroch Castle was really meant to be unique; standing on its elevated platform overlooking the city, it was destined to be a real show castle. While the descendants of some of the miners who once worked for the Dunsmuir Dynasty might not share this romantic view, there is something almost playful in its picturesque profile. In retrospect, this is as it should be, because the story of Craigdarroch is the legend of a rags to riches millionaire, who promised his sweetheart a castle if she would come with him to Canada — and she did.

DIRECTIONS: From downtown go north on Government Street; turn right on Fort Street; and then right again on to Joan Crescent. It is a 40 minute walk from the Inner Harbour.

Ashnola

IN THE SAME YEAR that Joan Dunsmuir moved into Craigdarroch, a ball was held at Cary Castle. It had been a long, hot summer in 1890, and Hugh Nelson was putting on a sumptuous party. Amongst the guests enjoying the Lieutenant Governor's hospitality that evening was a couple who attracted a lot of attention: he was a dashing young Englishman named Captain Northing Pinckney Snowden; and she was the former Emily Dunsmuir, one of eight daughters of Victoria's most celebrated family. The couple had married four years earlier, and had just moved into their own residence on the banks of the Gorge, a fashionable neighbourhood along a sheltered inlet in the city's west end. It was dubbed 'Ashnola Castle'. Captain Snowden, however, was a bit of a mystery.

Legend has it that Snowden sailed into Victoria in 1881. Nobody knows very much about his personal background, but evidently he lost no time in joining the Union Club. When he wasn't whacking cricket balls, he worked in Victoria as a real estate agent at the offices of Lowenberg and Harris, although he preferred to be known for his activities in the militia, where he served as adjutant in the gun battery of the Victoria Garrison Regiment. As well as firing weapons of mass destruction, Snowden took a keen interest in Victoria's social circles, and it was only a matter of time before he met Emily at a fancy dress party at Robert Dunsmuir's old residence of Fairview. Emily evidently took quite a liking to Captain Snowden—suitably dressed for the

Captain Northing Pinckney Snowden
BCA: 77981

occasion as a Turkish pasha—and he took quite a liking to Emily. They were married in 1886.

It was a magnificent ceremony. Emily looked charming as she was escorted confidently down the aisle of the old St. Andrew's Church by her father, Robert Dunsmuir. As the organ pealed forth the grand strains of the 'Wedding March', under the skilful expertise of Miss Anderson, a journalist from the *Colonist*, a newspaper never at a loss for words on such occasions, noted the bride's "elegant white satin dress, à la pompadour,

Emily Dunsmuir on her wedding day in 1886
BCA: E-00524

with honiton lace...[a] bridal veil and [a] mantle of orange blossoms." After the service, which was dutifully performed by the Reverend Mr. Stephens, the happy couple was whisked away to Fairview from where they embarked by steamer the following morning for their honeymoon in Yellowstone Park.

Ashnola Castle was presented to Emily by her father as a wedding gift. Built on 12 acres of property that Robert Dunsmuir had purchased from the Yates' estate in 1888, Ashnola was quite unique. It was situ-

Ashnola Castle
BCA: C-03809

ated on the Gorge opposite 'Burleith', the home of Emily's eldest brother, James Dunsmuir, and its construction created quite a stir among the local residents, who watched in awe as it rose majestically along the waterway. The architect was Leonard Buttress Trimen, an Englishman who had set up a practice in Victoria in the early 1880s, and who was noted for introducing the Gothic Vernacular Revival style to the city. Evidence of his work can still be seen in the newer St. Andrew's Church built on Douglas Street, a project funded in part by a generous donation from Robert Dunsmuir. Undoubtedly, it was Dunsmuir's familiarity with the architect's work that won Trimen the contract to build Ashnola, but the fact that his son-in-law was English, and not Scottish, possibly helps to explain the radical departure in Ashnola's design from Dunsmuir's previous projects. Even the castle's name (Ashnola) suggests a certain English gentility.

Trimen used an identical red-brick facade to the one he employed on St. Andrew's Church, but the circular turrets that are so prominent on St. Andrews, as well as Craigdarroch Castle, were conspicuously absent in the design of Ashnola. Instead, Ashnola incorporated a tall square tower, topped with a pointed metallic dome. Set near the entrance to the tower were the letters 'A' and 'C'; below was the letter 'S'. The latter might have signified 'Snowden', but the former remain a mystery. Two grand wings peeled off from behind the tower, each lined with fenestrations. A glass solar was built on one end of the residence, and a steep tiled roof capped with tall chimneys crowned the building. One feature quite evident at Ashnola was the light-coloured brickwork that decorated the edges of the structure—Trimen used a similar type of quoining on St. Andrew's Church, which can still be seen to this day on Douglas Street.

Ashnola was popularly dubbed a castle by local residents; however, it might more aptly be described as a Jacobean style mansion. Yet regardless of precisely what you called it, one fact is obvious: by the second generation, the Dunsmuir family was beginning to distance itself from its Scottish roots. A glimpse inside Ashnola Castle makes this abundantly clear. On entering the building, the visitor was greeted by a huge fireplace set in a wall of solid oak imported from England. In contrast, the dining room evoked a feeling of "delicacy and chasteness;" here could be found a colourful frieze of grape vines, embellished with wild roses and passion flowers, beneath a ceiling covered with doves. In the drawing room there was yet another frieze, "admirably disposed [with]...[r]oses, upon whose branches gold-finches had naturally disposed themselves." John R. Gilmer is credited with decorating the walls, but a German artist, William Schaefer, painted the ceilings; some critics concluded that this artwork was among the most elaborate ever conceived on the Pacific coast up until this period, surpassing even that found in Craigdarroch Castle.

Ashnola cost an estimated 25 000 dollars to build, although some historians have placed the final bill at 35 000 dollars. It was far less than Craigdarroch Castle, but considerably more than many of the other opulent homes being built in the neighbourhood at that time. 'The Dingle' [House], for example, a nearby Victorian Italianate residence built for Charles William Ringler Thomson, cost 9 000 dollars. However, Ashnola was made of stone, not wood, and this probably drove up the cost considerably. Moreover, much of the money spent on Ashnola Castle was devoted to landscaping the gardens.

Occupying 12 acres of property, the grounds were embellished with colourful flower beds set in a manicured lawn; the remaining meadows were marked off by a quaint iron fence imported from England. Behind the residence, on the water's edge, was Captain Snowden's private boat dock. But it was the front of the castle that created the most stunning impression. Guests approached the castle along an oval driveway of crushed white rock that swept up to the main door at the foot of the tower; on formal occasions, they were

The remains of Captain Snowden's boat dock on the Gorge
AUTHOR

announced in the Grand Hall by a butler. Ashnola was frequently the scene of garden parties, 'magical evenings' and formal dinners; but the grandest event of all was held on May 24, each year, when guests were invited to the castle to enjoy the celebrations marking Queen Victoria's birthday.

Captain Snowden had done very well for himself. After taking up residence at Ashnola, he began to act as though 'to the manor born', and he wasted no time in dreaming up new ways to spend the family fortune. Among his passions was travel: he and Emily frequently took trips to Europe, where Captain Snowden enjoyed shooting in the Scottish Highlands. Unfortunately, it was not to last. Captain Snowden left Victoria unexpectedly, and several years later his obituary suddenly appeared in the local newspaper, claiming that he had died in 1904 of injuries sustained in The Boer War.

No doubt this was how Captain Snowden would have liked to be remembered; unfortunately, he had been harbouring a dark secret. As a young man Snowden had contracted syphilis — a not uncommon affliction in those days — and although he believed the illness was in remission when he married Emily, he woke up one morning in bed at Ashnola Castle stark raving bonkers. Emily was forced to sell the residence to pay for her husband's medical expenses in England. The news wasn't all bad, however. Leaving Captain Snowden to die insane in the Holloway Sanitarium, Emily sailed back to Canada to live with her mother at Craigdarroch Castle. Fortunately, she was soon able to marry another Englishman named Henry Randall Burroughs — whence the nicely worded obituary in the local newspaper in 1904. Burroughs was from Norfolk, and Emily lived quite happily for another four decades, eventually dying in Ireland in 1944.

Ashnola Castle was not vacant for very long. It was sold in 1898 to a prominent local businessman named Edgar Crow Baker for 22 000 dollars. Fortunately, we know a little more about Mr. Baker's origins than we do about Captain Snowden's. Baker was born in 1843 in England, and entered the Royal Navy at the height of British sea power; a brilliant mathematician, he graduated first in his class of 400 cadets, and one of his earliest duties was to put down an insurrection in Jamaica. Later he helped to deal with the Fenian scare in Canada; finally, he ended up protecting the fishery in Newfoundland. Baker must have developed quite a

Edgar Crow Baker
BCA: 9391

fondness for Canada, because he subsequently left the Royal Navy, and immigrated to British Columbia. In 1873 he created the Province's first pilotage service; then, in 1882, he founded yet another venture, the Victoria and Esquimalt Telephone Company — the IT revolution of its day.

Like so many of Victoria's early businessmen, Baker served in the House of Commons. Then, in 1889, he decided to retire from politics to pursue his business interests. By all accounts Edgar Crow Baker was not only a successful businessman, but he was also an immensely popular man. A city directory in 1892 noted: "Mr. Baker is one of the most genial of men, an English gentleman in the truest sense of the word, a man of rare qualifications and extensive practical experience [and] highly esteemed by all classes of society."

Baker lived in the castle with his wife Marion for over twenty years. However, the Baker's made one important change: they renamed the castle 'Sissinghurst'. Baker, like so many denizens of Victoria's grand residences, probably felt a need to stamp his own imprimatur on the castle, but it clearly retained its English cachet. Although Edgar Crow Baker died in 1920, his wife Marion continued to live happily in Sissinghurst until 1944, when the residence was subsequently turned into a nursing home.

The castle was initially planned as a 25-bed hospital, but the facility was later expanded to 104 beds with the addition of the F.E. Winslow Wing at a cost of 450 000 dollars—nearly 20 times more than what Ashnola had originally cost to build. By this time its name had been changed yet again to the 'Gorge Road Hospital', and the ceiling of the old residence had been lowered, probably to conserve heat. A further expansion of the facility took place in 1961; unfortunately, a decade later a decision was made to tear down the old castle.

As far as the City was concerned, they were demolishing the castle in the name of progress; but, in retrospect, it was a deeply regrettable decision, and one that would never have been allowed today. On that fateful morning in 1971 a wrecking ball slammed into the building, and within minutes the tall tower stood alone amid the debris, teetering on the edge of collapse, until at last it too fell into the rubble in a cloud of dust. Not a trace of this glorious residence now remains. Ashnola Castle may be gone, but the memories linger. On a moonlit night you can still wander along the banks of the Gorge waterway, and make out the stone pilings

Marion Crow Baker in her lavishly furnished living room,
Sissinghurst, circa 1940
BCA: 05945

that were once the foundations of Captain Snowden's private boat dock. If you listen very carefully you might even hear the clink of champagne glasses and the sound of laugher; suddenly you will be carried back to an earlier time, when gaiety once filled the night air as the

Snowden's held one of those 'magical evenings' long ago at Ashnola Castle.

DIRECTIONS: *Ashnola once stood in the grounds of to-day's Gorge Road Hospital. From downtown go north on Government Street; then turn left on Gorge Road East; finally, turn left on Balfour Road. Walking not recommended. A 10 minute ride from the Inner Harbour.*

Government House

O N MAY 19, 1899, one year after Ashnola was sold to Edgar Crow Baker, the city awoke to a tragedy — Cary Castle was on fire. No one was more surprised than Lieutenant Governor Thomas Robert McInnes, who was forced to flee the burning building in his dressing gown, and take up temporary residence in a mansion on Moss Street. In the interim, speculation mounted as to the future of the site on top of Rockland Avenue: should a new residence be built to replace the old? Some said British Columbia couldn't afford a new home for the Lieutenant Governor; others said they didn't need one. In the end it was decided to rebuild the castle. George Hunter Cary would have been pleased.

Unfortunately, Government House was plagued with controversy from the start. It all began when the Provincial Government invited tenders to rebuild the residence. The task was awarded initially to a Vancouver firm; however, a Victoria architect objected to the proposal, saying he could rebuild Cary Castle for substantially less money if he were given the contract — his name was Francis Mawson Rattenbury. Rattenbury was already well known in British Columbia: he had built the Province's legislature in 1892, and four years later he designed the Bank of Montreal on Douglas Street.

Architect Francis Mawson Rattenbury in 1924
BCA: F-02163

His proposal was eventually accepted; nevertheless, in an attempt to deflect any impropriety he assigned an associate, Samuel Maclure, to act as the architect, while he retained the title of 'supervisory architect'. It took only two years to rebuild Government House, but the project was plagued by soaring costs, which embroiled Rattenbury in controversy for years. As it turned out, these 'striking irregularities' were the least of his problems.

Construction of Government House began in 1901, on the same site originally surveyed by Royal Engineers four decades earlier, amid the Garry Oaks and the glaciated rocks that led down to Ross Bay. Rattenbury chose a cross-axial floor plan. It comprised a central block with two wings that extended along an east-west axis from the main entrance (the porte-cochère was added several years later). Despite substantial changes, however, old Cary Castle was still evident in Rattenbury's new design. Although the drum-tower was replaced by a square keep, crenellations were retained, and imitation loops were added to the facade. Pointed arches were later incorporated into the porte-cochère, adding a Tudor touch. Some characterise the overall style of the new Cary Castle as Vernacular Revival. But perhaps the most outstanding feature was its Richardsonian-shingle exterior; it was a rather novel stylistic feature, and Rattenbury couldn't resist adding a set of tall Tudor chimneys. Rather less obvious was the roof. The castle was crowned with a hint of French Loire, a feature that Warren Heyward Williams had already flirted with in Craigdarroch Castle, but which would become much more prominent later in Rattenbury's design of the Empress Hotel. Nevertheless, if the exterior of the new Cary Castle owed much to Rattenbury, the interior was pure Maclure.

Rattenbury and Maclure came from rather different backgrounds. Born in England, Rattenbury immigrated to Canada in his early 20s, joined the Union Club, took out a membership in the Royal Victoria Yacht Club, and became a reeve in the Municipality of Oak Bay. By the time he built Government House, he was already recognised as British Columbia's premier institutional

The 'new' Cary Castle (Government House) in 1903
BCA: A-02784

designer with a particular fondness for the Chateau style of architecture. Samuel Maclure, by contrast, led a more private life. Born in Canada, the son of a Royal Engineer, Maclure was renowned for his meticulous attention to detail: his forte was the English half-timber idiom, and his signature is still to be seen in homes all over Victoria in the form of steep gables, magnificent halls, and dramatic staircases.

Both architects seem to have worked well together on this project, despite their differences. In many ways, their skills complemented one another. With the help of Spencer's Store, Maclure decorated the castle with Persian rugs, ottomans, antique tables and exquisite chairs, as well as expensive tapestries, many imported from England. Maclure also made liberal use of stained glass throughout the residence to take advantage of light streaming in through the tall windows. But the focal point of Government House was the enormous ballroom, a galleried hall decorated by James Bloomfield with images of native Indians; the ceiling, for example, was festooned with scenes from native legends, and the overall effect was stunning.

No one was more enamoured with the new 'gubernatorial' residence than the *Colonist*, which was pleased to report in 1901 that the "[w]indows [were] arranged in steps and their arrangement with the castellated cresting and ramparts at the tower tops [gave] the main entrance indeed a striking castle effect." By 1903 Government House was rapidly approaching completion, and it was no longer possible to complain bitterly, as some had once done, that Victorians were brought up in the backwoods, as if they had never seen homes built of stone. Unfortunately, there was a price to pay for this largesse. Although Rattenbury had won the competition by assuring the Ministry of Lands and Works that he could rebuild Cary Castle for less than his competitors, the final cost soared so high that Rattenbury was forced to appear before a parliamen-

tary committee to explain himself. Despite being offi-
cially exonerated of any blame, Government House was
completed under a cloud of controversy that lingered
for years. George Hunter Cary's restless spirit, it seems,
had not quite been put to rest.

Francis Mawson Rattenbury was not the only person to get into trouble, however. Before Lieutenant
Governor Thomas Robert McInnes could take up residence in his new castle he was ordered to pack his bags
and leave office. Temporarily living in a mansion on
Moss Street, McInnes was used to fleeing tall buildings
in a single bound. Unfortunately, this time it wasn't a
fire that drove him out, but his political indiscretion:
the dour Scot had been dabbling too liberally in politics, and the country's Prime Minister, Wilfrid Laurier,
was given little choice but to dismiss him.

His replacement was a Frenchman with the rather
convoluted title of The Honourable Lieutenant Governor Sir Henri-Gustave Joly de Lotbinière. Like his predecessor, the new Governor was forced to live on Moss
Street until Government House was finished; but it was
fortunate that he didn't have to wait too long, because
he had a very large family. Born in France, and until
recently a resident of Quebec, his wife had given birth
to no less than 11 children, a fact which may have con-
tributed to her untimely demise one year after her husband took office. In 1906, after barely three years at Government House, the Lieutenant Governor retired to
Quebec. The post was now vacant yet again.

In the years leading up to World War One, a succession of Lieutenant Governors occupied the new Cary
Castle. One was Sir James Dunsmuir. After retiring as

Premier of the Province, and having just fought a long and bitter legal battle with his mother for control of the

The Honourable Lieutenant Governor Henri-Gustave Joly de Lotbinère
BCA: 26063

family fortune, the coal baron was not overly eager to accept the appointment, but he eventually took the post at the insistence of his wife. James Dunsmuir was responsible for adding the porte-cochère to the entrance of Government House in 1909. His short tenure was

Built in 1909, the porte-cochère still graces
Government House
AUTHOR

followed by Thomas Wilson Paterson, under whose mandate the iron fence, and an imposing gate, were erected. This was a rather fortunate decision, because a riot broke out at the entrance to Government House in 1915 when an angry mob tried to storm the castle and attack the wife of Lieutenant Governor Francis Barnard — the daughter of a German brewer — after learning of the sinking of the Lusitania by a German submarine.

After the war further improvements were made to Government House: in 1912 the driveway was paved;

then, in 1927, Samuel Maclure put the finishing touches to the landscaping, shortly before dying later that year. For the next three decades the residence continued to serve as the home of various Lieutenant Governors, and visiting dignitaries, until tragedy struck once more. Like the old Cary Castle, Government House was a fire trap: faulty wiring, careless smokers, and a room full of celluloid film reels were all that were needed to ignite the conflagration. Early on the morning of April 15, 1957, fire broke out at Government House yet again, consuming the castle, and forcing Lieutenant Governor Frank

Driveway leading into Government House
AUTHOR

Ross to flee the burning building in his pajamas. George Hunter Cary had struck once more. No sooner had the hot embers cooled down, however, than the Province rebuilt the residence: but after spending 1 600 000 dollars on the new building, all traces of Cary Castle disappeared — except for the elegant porte-cochère, which survived the fire and which still stands at the entrance to the new residence today. Unfortunately, the battlements on the roof have vanished, and nowadays Government House resembles a large ski chalet. George Hunter Cary would not be amused.

Francis Mawson Rattenbury would probably be equally disappointed. One gets the impression that he was a rather cantankerous individual, whose confidence was often mistaken for arrogance. After completing Government House, he went on to build the Empress Hotel, a formidable undertaking, which gave full rein to his passion for the chateauesque by combining a French Loire roof with an English medieval facade. Unfortunately, he had a disagreement with the president of the Canadian Pacific Railway Company, Thomas George Shaughnessy, over the interior design of the hotel, and he resigned two years before the project was completed.

From then on it was all downhill for Rattenbury. Several years after completing his pièce-de-résistance, he stunned the Victoria establishment by abandoning his wife for a younger woman. Her name was Alma Victoria Clarke Dolling Pakenham. It proved an unhappy liaison: shunned by the city's establishment, the couple eventually retired to England, where Rattenbury was murdered in 1937 by his chauffeur in what turned out to be a ménage-à-trois, involving him, Alma, and the young driver — George Percy Stoner. Stoner's death sentence was later commuted to a long term of penal servitude, but by this time Alma had stabbed herself to death in a fit of anguish. It would be a slight exaggeration to call Rattenbury a genius, but he certainly left an indelible mark on Victoria's urban landscape in more ways than one. The city just wouldn't be the same without Ratz.

Samuel Maclure's life was a stark contrast to the tumultuous career of Francis Mawson Rattenbury. Although Maclure suffered from illness throughout much of his life, dying ten years earlier than Rattenbury, he was in many ways more fortunate. Maclure was certainly less controversial. Part of the reason for his success was the growing realisation that by the turn of the last century Victoria was developing a reputation as a place of picturesque gardens, leisure activities, and retirement opportunities. Rudyard Kipling captured this spirit when he visited the city in 1907, describing it as being rather like "Bournemouth with the Himalayas in the background." Inevitably, as more people settled in Victoria, the demand for private residences climbed. If Rattenbury was British Columbia's premier institutional architect, however, Maclure was the Province's premier residential architect, and in the end it was Maclure, and not Rattenbury, who was to build the grandest residence of all — Hatley Park.

DIRECTIONS: The new Cary Castle once stood on the grounds of today's Government House. From Downtown go north on Government Street; turn right on to Fort street; turn right on Cook Street; then make an immediate left turn on to Rockland Avenue. Gardens are open from sunrise to sunset. It is a 45 minutes walk from the Inner Harbour.

Hatley Park

HATLEY CASTLE is by far the most exquisite residence ever built in western Canada. But in contrast to Craigdarroch Castle, which overlooks the city in a very conspicuous setting, Hatley sits on a far more secluded site in a heavily wooded area in Colwood known as Hatley Park. For one of North America's wealthiest industrialists, a man who had been a Premier of the Province, a Lieutenant Governor, and the recipient of a knighthood, Sir James Dunsmuir chose a very quiet life in his later years: conspicuous consumption in the Dunsmuir family had finally given way to a need for private indulgence — at least for James Dunsmuir.

James Dunsmuir was born in 1851, the eldest son of a family of two boys and eight girls. It was always understood that he and his brother Alex would play a pivotal role in the family business, and with this in mind James was sent to study mining at a college in Virginia. It was here that he met his future wife, the vivacious Laura Surles, a woman from the plantation aristocracy of North Carolina, who had family connections to the famous Byrd family. The couple married on July 5, 1876, at the Old Sardis Church in Cumberland County, and then enjoyed their honeymoon on the way back to Vancouver Island where they began their new life together.

By all accounts James was a diligent worker, and he and his brother Alex gradually assumed more responsibility as their father grew older. Robert Dunsmuir had promised to leave his sons the business on his death, and both brothers laboured under that assumption. But when the coal baron died, leaving all his wealth to his wife, the brothers became embroiled in a bitter legal battle with their mother that tore the family apart: Joan and her daughters fought to retain the family fortune; James and Alex tried to wrestle it from them. The battle did not end until 1906, by which time Alex was dead, James was exhausted, and his mother was so angry that she never spoke to her son again. It was a bittersweet victory for James Dunsmuir. But it wasn't all bad news.

Several years after the death of Robert Dunsmuir, James and Laura moved into Burleith, an enormous Queen Anne style mansion overlooking the Gorge opposite the residence of Emily and Captain Snowden. As a result of the ongoing legal battle between James Dunsmuir and his own mother, the relationship with Emily was probably rather strained. Nevertheless, in 1900 James Dunsmuir did become Premier of the Province. He was not a gifted debater, but he was careful not to make the political blunders of his father by suggesting that British Columbia join the United States. By contrast, Laura was a consummate entertainer at Burleith, and made the most of her husband's political appointment by hosting a list of dignitaries, among them the Duke and Duchess of York. In 1906, the year James Dunsmuir finally won his much publicised lawsuit against his own mother, he capped off his career

The Honourable Lieutenant Governor Sir James Dunsmuir
BCA: A-01246

by being sworn in as the new Lieutenant Governor of the Province. But it was an honour he reluctantly accepted at the insistence of his wife. By then, James Dunsmuir was seriously contemplating retirement;

given the vicissitudes of his tumultuous life, it is hardly surprising that he sought some privacy.

It was while serving as Lieutenant Governor that James Dunsmuir began to purchase property near Colwood for a new residence in preparation for his retirement. According to the Land Titles' Office, he bought the first 250 acres in 1907 from Roland Stuart for the tidy sum of 50 000 dollars; several more purchases followed, eventually amounting to nearly 800 acres of property. His plan was to create a private estate that would supply all its own needs through agriculture. But James Dunsmuir didn't only want to become a gentleman farmer, he also wanted enough property to indulge himself in his passion for hunting and fishing. The only question that remained was what type of residence should he build? If Laura had her way, the home might have resembled a 'Gone with the Wind' mansion; but, like his father before him, James wanted a castle — and a castle it was to be.

Similar to Ashnola, Hatley Castle is in many ways a rejection of the family's Scottish roots: its martial face has a distinctly Anglo-Norman look about it. Several factors probably account for this departure in design. There is some evidence that James' eldest son, 'Robin' Dunsmuir, suggested that the family model the castle on an English country seat. But the fact that James Dunsmuir was residing at Government House in the years leading up to the construction of Hatley Castle must also be taken into consideration. There is no doubt that James Dunsmuir was enamoured by the new Cary Castle — even if he had been reluctant to accept the position of Lieutenant Governor — because in 1909 he paid for the construction of its porte-cochère, an addition which stands at the entrance to Government House to this day. Undoubtedly, Dunsmuir's sojourn at Government House from 1906-1909 influenced his choice of design for his own retirement residence, because there

View of Hatley Castle from the north
AUTHOR

are unmistakable parallels between the two castles. Nevertheless, the influence of the architect is also an important consideration.

It is interesting to note that Rattenbury was not chosen by the Dunsmuirs to be the architect of Hatley. Rattenbury was probably available; unfortunately, the parliamentary investigation into the supervisory architect's expenditures at Government House, and his inability to reconcile differences between himself and some of his clients, may well have made the Dunsmuirs more disposed towards his colleague, Samuel Maclure. Laura would certainly have been impressed with the interior design of the new Cary Castle, and this would also have boded well for Maclure. But in the end it might simply have boiled down to personality. Like James Dunsmuir, Maclure was born in Canada — New Westminster to be precise; moreover, he was closer to Dunsmuir's own age. Consequently, James Dunsmuir may well have considered Maclure not only to be a more stable individual, but also a more agreeable man with whom to do business. But one nagging question still remained: precisely what should the castle look like?

The solution came from a most unexpected source. In Samuel Maclure's employ were two young brothers, Douglas and Percy Leonard James, each of whom had recently emigrated from the Old Country. During his apprenticeship in England, Douglas James had sketched the seat of the Countess of Warwick, a 16th-century manor house called 'Compton Wynyates'. The word 'wynyates' means 'windy valley' in Old English. Historians are reasonably certain that Samuel Maclure's design for Hatley Castle was based in part upon this fortified English manor house in Warwickshire; even the name of the Dunsmuir's castle was probably imported directly form England: one researcher, for example, has discovered that the name 'Hatley' appears three times on the map between Biggleswade and Cambridge. But experts all agree that Samuel Maclure was not a copyist — he had his own inimitable style, and this is clearly evident in the design of Hatley Castle.

Samuel Maclure was noted for his meticulous attention to detail, and nearly 250 preparatory sketches were made of Hatley Castle. Its design was based on a crosss-axial floor plan with a castellated block at the centre and a Tudoresque wing attached to each end. Aligned along an east-west axis, the castle is best viewed from the main entrance on the north side. Dominating the residence from this angle is a central tower, resembling a medieval keep, which is flanked by two octagonal turrets; a third turret rises majestically above the

View of Hatley from the northeast
AUTHOR

Great Tower on its western edge. A porte-cochère, reminiscent of Government House, was added to the main entrance, and this entire portion of the residence is heavily decorated with castellations, corbels and imitation loops. On either side of the central block are the Tudor wings, whose most conspicuous features are the steeply fretted gables that adorn the roof line — Samuel Maclure's signature. Viewed from the south, however, the central block is now encrusted with ivy, and its symmetrical facade is broken by oriels, angular gables, and Tudor chimney pots, lending the residence an Edwardian appearance. On each side of the Tudor wings can clearly be seen the octagonal turrets, offset at an angle, and capped with corbels and more battlements. The roof itself is made of slate, imported from Westmoreland.

What is most remarkable about Hatley, however, is that it took only 18 months to build: construction began in 1908, and the building was finished by 1910. The general contractor was Mr. Catterall, a man well known to the Dunsmuirs — his company built both Craigdarroch Castle and Ashnola Castle. Catterall used locally quarried granite for the walls, but Andesite Sandstone was employed for all the sills, mullions and copings; the masonry on the central tower, for example, is 3' 6" thick. The overall effect is stunning.

Yet even more interesting is the subtle way in which the overall design gives the impression that the castle was built over a long period of time. Specifically, the central block seems much older than the wings, as if the Tudor additions were later built on to a medieval castle. Ivy, clinging to the walls on the south side of the residence, further augments the appearance of age. In overall appearance, Hatley really does resemble the country seat of a family that traces its lineage much further back than just two generations. It is as if the home is meant to distance the Dunsmuir family from their humble origins, and legitimise their wealth. The fact that James Dunsmuir chose not to replicate the castle of a Scottish laird, but instead adopted an Anglo-Norman design, is also perhaps indicative of his desire to transform his family image.

Evidently James Dunsmuir succeeded. In 1910 the *Colonist* glowingly compared Hatley to Blenheim Pal-

A stone plaque on the north wall reveals
the castle's date of construction: '1908'
AUTHOR

ace. Unfortunately, it had not been achieved without some difficulties. Samuel Maclure found himself in the rather unenviable position of constantly having to reconcile James Dunsmuir's demands for a country retreat, where he could indulge himself in hunting and fishing, with Laura's passion for entertaining. By setting the residence in nearly 800 acres of woodland, and giving the home a martial face, Samuel Maclure was certainly catering to the tastes of the former; but the Edwardian additions and the elegant gardens must have pleased the lady of the house. The interior of the residence, however, was particularly challenging for Samuel Maclure. A look inside the castle illustrates why.

The main entrance to the residence is on the north side of the castle. Here the visitor walks underneath the porte-cochère, ascends a flight of stone steps, and then enters the castle through a heavy oak door. The spacious wood-panelled hall is illuminated by a phalanx of windows above a minstrel gallery that floods the scene with daylight, highlighting the rich texture of

View of Hatley from the northwest
AUTHOR

the carpet. Dominating the hall is a huge fireplace made of Arizona Sandstone, above which hangs the head of an enormous stag that was purportedly shot by James Dunsmuir on one of his hunting expeditions. The woodwork of the Tudor Hall is exquisite. Over 25 carpenters were employed by Dixon and Howes during the construction of Hatley Castle, but the fine detailing was the work of a craftsman named George Gibson, who helped to create the Arts and Crafts motif that is evident throughout the building.

Turning left, and walking down the main corridor, the visitor comes to the east wing. At the far end is the kitchen. In its day the kitchen was filled with modern appliances and a series of bells that alerted the staff as to which room in the castle was requesting their service. Next door is the dining room. The dining room is fashioned from quartered oak, but the floor is solid teak with an Australian bean wood trim. Light streaming in through the windows highlights the stained glass, which is inscribed with Roman mythology. Laura Dunsmuir took the liberty of having a footpedal installed in the floor so that she could discretely summon the servants at the end of each course — Laura took her entertaining very seriously. Moving farther west along the corridor, the visitor reaches the drawing room. The drawing room is bright and spacious, and overlooks a veranda with the Olympic Mountains in the distance. Curiously, by placing the kitchen and dining area in the east wing, and locating the living quarters in the west of the building, the design follows a similar floor plan to a medieval castle.

Walking farther along the carpeted corridor, the building assumes a more masculine tone. It is here that Samuel Maclure built the library. The library is a small room that is inscribed with masonic symbols that attest to James Dunsmuir's affiliation with freemasonry. On the other side of the corridor is the billiard room, which still boasts the original table. It was here that the Prince of Wales was once rumoured to have shot a bullet hole in the ceiling. Actually, it was an adjoining alcove, and it wasn't the Prince, but James Dunsmuir—he accidentally let loose his shotgun after he came in from a day of hunting on his estate. At the extreme west end of the main floor is James Dunsmuir's office, a dark-panelled room, adorned with yacca wood from Fiji and jarrah

Castellated oriel on the north side
of the castle
AUTHOR

wood from Australia. For the fabulous Dunsmuirs, it seems, no expense was spared.

Climbing the twin staircase to the second floor, the visitor finds the family bedrooms. James and Laura had two sons, and eight daughters; however, much of

James Dunsmuir's time was spent avoiding the women by retreating to his office, or hunting and fishing on his estate. The children's rooms were once heavily wallpapered — a popular custom in Edwardian times — but the largest rooms were reserved for the sons. Jimmie, or 'Boy' as he was nicknamed, even had his own valet. The Dunsmuir's bedroom overlooks the Straits of Juan de Fuca, and it was in this room that Laura died in 1937. Climbing higher still, the visitor reaches the third floor, where guests once slept. Finally, ascending one more flight of steps, one reaches the top floor, which was designed to be a ballroom. This is a bit of a mystery: people often wonder why the ballroom was placed on the top floor of the castle. Nevertheless, it follows a similar model already established in the design of Craigdarroch Castle. To assist in the entertainment of his guests, James Dunsmuir stocked his wine cellar with copious amounts of port and claret, not to mention all that wine.

In total there are 40 rooms in Hatley Castle, but despite its scale the exquisite attention to detail was never compromised. The stained glass windows, for example, were imported from William Morris and Company of England, and fireplaces still adorn many of the rooms, each one decorated in its original Neoclassical style. Outside, even the drain pipes are a work of art, having been specially cast in Glasgow, and inscribed with a florid rendering of the year '1908', the date the castle was built. Laura was equally attentive to the furnishings: the original pieces were purchased under the guidance of Samuel Maclure, many of them at great expense, when the architect accompanied Laura on a buying spree through the capitals of Europe during the final stages of construction. By the time the Dunsmuirs moved into Hatley in 1910 this lavish residence had be-

An ornate drain pipe
near the main entrance
AUTHOR

come home to nearly 30 people, which included not only the Dunsmuir family, but a staff of cooks and servants, as well as a tutor, an English nanny, a butler, a foot-man, and a chauffeur.

Yet Hatley was still not finished. The ambitious project of landscaping the grounds of Hatley Park was given to the firm Brett and Hall of Boston. A curved driveway first had to be built to sweep up to the porte-cochère at the main entrance of the castle. Next, a series of cascading steps were constructed that led down the steep embankment to the front door; originally intended to be a waterfall, they soon acquired the sobriquet 'Neptune's Steps'. An Italianate garden with a Florentine arbor was then built near the west wing, and a croquet lawn was added to an adjoining lawn. The Dunsmuirs were still not finished, however.

Natural streams flowed through the grounds, and a series of pools were created that led down to the sea. Isaburo Kishita came to Canada specifically to build the Japanese garden beside one of the pools, which includes an island teahouse. But the Dunsmuirs' pièce-de-résistance was the conservatory, an enormous glass

Elegant stone figurine
in the Italian garden
AUTHOR

solarium, stocked with exotic plants from all over the world. It was Canada's answer to Kew Gardens. The conservatory was custom built for the Dunsmuirs' estate by Lord and Burnham of Philadelphia, although the glass was imported from France. It cost a staggering 75 000 dollars to build, and consumed almost as much coal as the Titanic. But there was no shortage of energy in the Dunsmuir family.

The Japanese garden, designed by Isaburo Kishita
AUTHOR

It had been James Dunsmuir's intention to farm the land at Hatley Park. Clearly, a certain degree of compromise had to be reached between the aesthetic issues of landscaping, and the more practical needs of agriculture. With this in mind, six miles of roads were eventually built on the estate, and a dairy, a slaughterhouse and a stable were erected. At its peak, the farm employed 120 Chinese labourers — discretely housed in their own small village of course. Yet, despite having to perform menial work, it was safer than working underground in one of the Dunsmuirs' coal mines. John Graham was appointed manager of the estate, and he lived in a gatehouse at the entrance to Hatley Park. Unfortunately, the farm was never profitable.

If the north side of the castle had a rather utilitarian air about it, the south side was more picturesque: here, meadows led down to Esquimalt Lagoon, the Straits of Juan de Fuca, and the Olympic Mountains beyond. The remainder of the estate, however, was left as wilderness. When James Dunsmuir finally erected a wall around the property in 1913, he effectively built a bailey, creating a kind of medieval fiefdom complete with its own village of Chinese labourers. The Dunsmuirs had come a long way in just two generations.

Ironically, James Dunsmuir's first imperial act was abdication. No sooner had he moved into Hatley than he began to sell off his businesses one by one, converting them into liquid assets. Unlike his father, James intended to enjoy the family fortune. The woods around Hatley Park were filled with deer, and the streams leading down to the sea were stocked with trout and wild salmon. Not content to merely indulge himself in his passion for hunting and fishing on his estate, he even had a lodge built for himself on the Cowichan River, which can still be seen standing today. But his pride and joy was *Dolaura*, a private yacht built for a reported 200 000 dollars, and launched from a shipyard on the Clyde. At the end of the Second World War it was used to ferry Jews to the British Mandate of Palestine, but in 1908 James Dunsmuir travelled to Europe to attend its maiden voyage. One evening, while moored in the Kiel

Ship Canal, an imperious looking German officer in a naval uniform marched on board to take a closer look at the vessel—it was Kaiser Wilhelm. The world was beginning to take note of the fabulous Dunsmuirs.

Historians tend to agree, however, that despite all his wealth James Dunsmuir was not a terribly inspiring individual. Sombre and morose in public, he did little to hide his contempt for labour, and enjoyed nothing better than hunting, fishing and male companionship. After spending much of his life in the shadow of his father, fighting his mother for control of the family business, and then serving reluctantly as both a Premier and as a Lieutenant Governor of the Province, his desire for privacy is hardly surprising. Retirement must have come as a welcome relief. Laura Dunsmuir, by contrast, was just the opposite.

James Dunsmuir's wife led a very active social life, and was happiest entertaining. While her pipe-smoking husband liked to escape to the Union Club, Laura eagerly participated in philanthropic organisations like the Alexandria Club, attended the local church in Colwood and, of course, acted as the chatelaine of Hatley Castle. One gets the impression that Hatley Park was Laura's 'Field of Dreams': "Build it and they will come," she must have thought—and come they did. Over the next two decades dignitaries flocked to Hatley Park from all over the world, among them the Prince of Wales, Winston Churchill, and several of Canada's Governor Generals, including Lord Tweedsmuir and Vincent Massey. But being the richest family in western Canada didn't shield the Dunsmuirs from tragedy. Five years after moving into Hatley fate dealt the family a cruel blow from which they never fully recovered.

In 1914 the lights went out all over Europe. The *Dolaura* was put on active service in the waters around Vancouver Island, and James Dunsmuir's 21 year old son 'Boy' enlisted in the army. In the years leading up to the war, Boy had led a rather pampered life. He was an outstanding horseman, and spent much of his time riding at Hatley Park. While still in his teens, he accompanied his parents on a tour of the Continent, travelled to Egypt, and even studied at Versailles with a private tutor, before returning to Canada, where he took up a position with the Bank of Montreal. Evidently Boy found banking rather dull work, and he became so impatient to see action that he sailed for England to join a British cavalry regiment.

Unfortunately, Boy bought a ticket on the Lusitania. Sailing under an American flag, the ship was supposedly protected from hostile interference; besides, it was considered too fast to be torpedoed by an enemy submarine. But the Lusitania was rumoured to be carrying munitions. The German Admiralty took a rather dim view of neutral ships supporting England in the war effort, and warned that it intended to retaliate against all shipping. On that fateful afternoon, as the Lusitania neared the coast of Ireland, it was suddenly torpedoed by a German submarine lurking near the entrance to the English Channel. The liner sank within minutes, and hundreds of passengers drowned, among them James Dunsmuir's son. Boy's body was never identified. It was ironic that only a few years earlier James Dunsmuir had stood on the deck of the *Dolaura* in the Kiel Ship Canal, and had shaken the hand of the Kaiser. Now the Kaiser had stolen the apple of his eye.

A dark cloud descended upon Hatley Park: James and Laura Dunsmuir were both so devastated by the news of their son's death that they withdrew from public life almost entirely. James never did recover. Part of his disappointment lay in the fact that it had always been expected that Boy would manage the family fortune after his father's death. It was not a responsibility that James dared to leave to his older son, Robert.

'Robin', as he was known, was very different to Boy. Robin was 17 years older than his brother; he married a girl from a wealthy family in Sausalito, California, with the rather unusual name of Maude Allingham Shoobert. But this promising beginning was not to last. Robin's inept handling of the family business was apparent from the start: once when his father asked him to travel to Denman Island to assist in the salvage of a ship that had run aground with a cargo of coal, Robin arrived late after spending the company's money in a drinking binge with 'the boys' in Nanaimo. It was clear that Robin was an alcoholic just like his Uncle Alex.

It wasn't that Robin lacked potential. It was just that his grand schemes always seemed to go awry after scaring away potential investors with his heavy drinking. Throughout his life, it was as if Robin constantly needed to prove himself his father's equal, even after losing the latter's confidence in his ability to manage the family fortune. Ultimately, he failed to win his father's approval, but he never stopped trying: Robin spent much of his life travelling across South American attempting to persuade governments to let him build them railroads. In spite of his lack of success, his adventures were not without their comical moments.

On his way to Argentina in 1910, for example, Robin stopped in San Francisco where he met a woman

Dunsmuir family, circa 1908 (Back, L to R: Robin, his wife Maude, John Hope, unidentified man, Arthur Bromley, Maye, Guy Audain. Middle: Bessie, Laura Dunsmuir, Boy, James Dunsmuir, Byrdie. Front: Marion, Kathleen, Dola, Jimmy Audain, Elinor, Muriel)
BCA: H-02835

named Dorothy Russell in a waterfront hotel called 'The Breakers' Inn'. His Uncle Alex would have probably still recognised the place. 'Dottie', as she was popularly known to the locals, was entertaining the crew of a U.S. destroyer by performing an undulating Turkish dance for which she required a great deal of room˙ — the crew then reciprocated. Rumours circulated that the pair married, although they never actually used the Dunsmuir name. On reaching South America, however, Robin then took up with another woman, an English girl he met in Buenos Aires called Florence Swindon; the prodigal son caused quite a stir when he brought her back to Victoria and made her his wife. By this time his marriage to Maude had been dissolved, and the unfortunate woman was quietly repatriated to California with enough money to protect the Dunsmuir name. In 1922, Robin concocted yet another wild scheme—this time with the Peruvian Government—but like all his previous business ventures, it soon fell apart. Tragically, Robin died in 1929 in a second-rate hotel in Singapore, fulfilling his father's prophecy.

Fortunately, James Dunsmuir didn't live long enough to see this sad day. One night in 1920, after a day of fishing on the Cowichan River, he went to bed in his lodge and never woke up—he was 69 years old. Without an heir apparent to the Dunsmuir Dynasty, James left his estate to Laura. But of the 15 million dollars once estimated to make up the family fortune, much of it had gone into building Hatley Park; the remainder had been spent over the years on expensive wedding gifts, holidays in Europe and, of course, those heavy legal bills from the years of family squabbling. By the time James Dunsmuir died, his estate was worth a little over 3 million dollars—much of it in bonds. Although Laura could still live out her days in luxury, the Dunsmuir family was soon to suffer yet another blow.

The very forces that had helped expand global capitalism now revealed an underlying weakness in the economy. In 1929 the stock market reacted violently, and within days it became painfully clear that the Wall Street Crash had reduced many of Laura's investments to nothing. The Dunsmuirs, like so many investors, never knew what hit them. It wasn't quite as grim as it first appeared, however; after all, this was the Great Depression, and deflation made money go a lot further than in the Roaring Twenties. Nevertheless, one immediate result of the Crash was to reduce the size of the Chinese labour force on the estate. As well as attempting to make agriculture more productive during the next few years, Kathleen, one of Laura's eight daughters, even tried launching a film career using the family estate as a backdrop.

In 1933 she made her first attempt. Unfortunately, 'Mystery of Harlow Manor' was a thriller that never quite got off the ground. But 'Crimson Paradise' was a little more successful. Filmed on location at Hatley Castle, Butchart Gardens and Beacon Hill Park at a cost of nearly 60 000 dollars, it was based on the book *The Crimson West* by Alexander Philip: the story is about a young Vancouver man who goes to the Cariboo, falls in love, and has to win a girl's hand by challenging a burly logger. Of course, brawn is no match for brains, but the film was a box office flop anyway, despite trying to win over an American audience by rewriting a rich Bostonian university graduate into the script. After banging on the doors of Hollywood without success, Kathleen finally took her lawyer's advice, and left the film business for good. Tragically, she died in the London Blitz in 1941 at the Café de Paris—a night club modelled, ironically, on the Palm Room of the Lusitania, the same ship that had claimed the life of her brother in 1915.

By this time the matriarch of Hatley Park was also dead. Laura died quietly in her bedroom overlooking the Olympic Mountains in 1937—she was 80 years old. Laura left an estate valued at 2 334 903 dollars, but as with Craigdarroch Castle a generation earlier the

Hatley Castle from the southwest, taken from the croquet lawn
AUTHOR

contents of Hatley Castle were quickly auctioned off by her surviving daughters, and the home was put up for sale. The asking price was a modest 260 000 dollars; however, despite running advertisements in *Country Life* and *Mayfair* in England, there were no serious offers. Interestingly, King George VI and Queen Elizabeth visited the castle in 1939, and for a brief time it was considered a possible home for the Royal Family in the event that England fell victim to the Jackboot. But this was not necessary. Instead, Hatley Park was purchased by the Royal Canadian Navy in 1940 for 75 000 dollars, and became a military college. It was a ridiculous price, but it was not without a touch of irony: the navy had bought the coal which built the Dunsmuir Dynasty nearly a century earlier; it was only fitting that the grandest home ever built by the Dunsmuirs should be sold back to them at a bargain price.

In retrospect, Robert Dunsmuir made the money, James Dunsmuir managed it, and the children spent it. The girls lost it all within a generation — Los Angeles, London, Paris and Monte Carlo were among the daughters' favourite haunts. It was here that they mixed with movie stars, millionaires and Russian 'counts', frequenting the world's most lavish casinos, while sipping champagne, and admiring each others jewellery. One by one they died off as the Dunsmuir fortune slowly ebbed away like a receding tide. Some, like Emily, came home to die: today she rests in the family plot at Ross Bay Cemetery beside the ashes of her sister, Kathleen, who was killed in the Café de Paris in London. Marion chose Monte Carlo. Dola was the last of her generation to go.

Born in 1903, Dola was the youngest child in the family. She was seven when the Dunsmuirs moved to Hatley Park, but although Dola enjoyed an enviable childhood, one gets the impression that she was not a happy woman. Dola was married, briefly, to a naval officer named Cavendish, whose family traced its pedigree back to a lesser branch of the distinguished Devonshire family. Their childless relationship was dissolved in 1933, although Dola did return to Canada to help raise Kathleen's children after their mother was killed in London in World War Two.

All her life Dola was shy, self-conscious and a rather unattractive woman, and perhaps it was her sense of insecurity that drew her into a lifelong relationship with another woman — the actress Tallulah Bankhead. Tallulah was everything Dola was not. Attractive, vivacious, and prone to scandal, Tallulah thrived on a combination of sex, drugs and alcohol. Asked once by one of Hollywood's most salacious gossip columnists, Earl Wilson, if she had ever been mistaken for a man on the telephone, she replied, "no darling, have you?" Tallulah is rumoured to have smoked over 100 cigarettes a day and drank copious amounts of bourbon — Dola preferred warm gin. By 1964, their rocky relationship was coming to an end; in that year passengers were shocked to see a hysterical Dola sobbing goodbye to Tallulah at Victoria's airport, crying because she would never see her again. She never did. The poor little rich girl died two years later. Evidently Dola declined a spot in the family crypt, preferring instead to be buried in St. John the Baptist Church in Colwood, a building paid for in part by a generous donation from her mother in 1912.

Despite the Dunsmuirs very public lives, there are still a few skeletons in the closet. Rumours still circulate that Dola was the illegitimate offspring of James Dunsmuir's eldest son, Robin, and a servant at Burleith who has never been identified. It's an intriguing theory. Robin would have been 26 when Dola was born, and knowing what we know about his very public private

life such a situation would not be impossible. Moreover, for Laura Dunsmuir to have given birth to Dola,
she would have had to be 45 years old at the time. In
1903, when Dola was born, James and Laura Dunsmuir
were living at Burleith, and James would have just completed two very short years as Premier of the Province.
Did James Dunsmuir suddenly cut short his tenure as
Premier to deal with this embarrassing situation at home
perhaps? In those days, without intense media scrutiny, it would certainly have been possible. But although
we will never know for certain, the private papers of
Laura express her affections for Dola in a way that certainly cast doubt on this hypothesis.

Descendants of the Dunsmuirs still live in Victoria, but the history of the family really ends with Dola.
However, this was not the end of Hatley Park. In 1995,
after the military college finally closed due to budget
cuts by the Federal Government, the castle reinvented
itself as Royal Roads University, an institution of higher
learning that specialises in innovative courses through
distance learning. Ironically, film studios still visit
Hatley Castle on a regular basis, and Kathleen would
be delighted to know that these productions actually
make money. Speaking of money, James Dunsmuir
would be shocked to learn today that his castle, which
reputedly cost him about a million dollars to build, has
recently been appraised at 100 million; the entire estate
is estimated to be worth a staggering quarter of a bil-
lion dollars! And unlike the other castles that were built
in Victoria, it even has a ghost.

The 'Lady in White' first appeared to cadets when
the castle was a tri-service military college. Apparently,

she would walk through the castle at night, and then glide out of the window. 'Annabelle', as she is known, was a servant of the Dunsmuir household who committed suicide by leaping from a third floor window on learning that the sailor from Port Angeles whom she was about to wed was already married. The 'Lady in White' has been seen on numerous occasions, often accompanied by other strange events such as a cool breeze, the sound of music, and the slamming of doors. Other ghosts have also been reported over the years, including that of Laura Dunsmuir. The university takes these matters so seriously that nowadays women are not required to work on the third floor of the castle alone after dark. The legacy of the Dunsmuirs, it seems, lingers on: even in death they exert a strange fascination over the living. But perhaps that is not surprising given the pivotal role that the family played on Canada's imperial margins. One thing is certain, however, Hatley Park is no ghost; the castle remains today one of the finest homes ever built, and it stands as a lasting symbol of a family that in only three generations made a fortune, and then spent it.

DIRECTIONS: *You will need transportation to reach Hatley Park – now known as Royal Roads University. From downtown go north on Government Street; turn left on Johnson Street; once over the Johnson Street Bridge the road turns into Tyee, then Skinner and, finally, Craigflower Road. Follow the road signs to Colwood. Once through the town centre turn left into Royal Roads University. It is a 25 minute ride from the Inner Harbour.*

Spencer Castle

HATLEY PARK certainly represents the apogee of the castle building era on Canada's imperial margins, but it was not the last residence to incorporate a martial facade. In 1912 yet another castle was built in Victoria, this time at the top of Cook Street on a windswept promontory overlooking the city. Now known as Spencer Castle, it was once the home of the architect who built it. His name was Henry Sandham Griffith and, like the architects who preceded him, his impact upon Victoria's urban landscape was considerable.

Griffith was born at Aston Vicarage, Oxfordshire, in 1865. After attending Christ Church College, Oxford, he began work at the firm of Webb and Tubb in Reading. Following in the footsteps of so many Englishmen, he immigrated to Canada in the early 1890s, and opened an architectural practice first in Winnipeg, and then in Saskatoon, before finally settling in Victoria in 1905. According to one architectural historian: "[His] commercial work exhibited [a] fine sense of proportion combined with a sensitive handling of Edwardian classical decoration." One of his most impressive commissions in Victoria was the Times Building; however, Spencer Castle is the building for which he is perhaps best remembered.

Several factors probably motivated Griffith to build himself a castle. His English heritage, a familiarity with Gothic Revivalism, and his personal wealth were obvious factors, but he may also have been inspired by some of the castles already prominent in Victoria. By the beginning of the 20th century, nearly half a dozen castles had been built in the city, among them, Cary Castle, Armadale Castle, Craigdarroch Castle, Ashnola Castle, and, more recently, Hatley Castle. Griffith must have been particularly impressed with the latter, and Spencer Castle may have been an attempt to emulate James Dunsmuir's residence—albeit on a smaller scale. Neverthless, it is also important to note that Griffith deeply admired the work of his contemporary, Samuel Maclure, and it is no accident that Spencer Castle incorporates traces of Tudor-Revivalism into its design.

Griffith selected a location for his residence on Smith's Hill, once sacred to local Indians who practised a form of divination in a nearby pond. Construction began in 1912. Like Hatley Castle, which Samuel Maclure had just completed, Spencer Castle is modelled on a cross-axial floor plan, although the imposing keep is not centred, but deliberately offset on the east wing. The castle is partially built of local granite, and is aligned on an east-west axis: it combines steep gables along the roof line with a balustraded terrace; and its martial face is enhanced by a three-storey tower capped with imitation corbels, merlons and embrasures. Combining a

Spencer Castle from the road on the south side of the building
AUTHOR

half-timber idiom with heavy stone massing, the overall style parallels the English Gothic Revival Vernacular, with prominent Georgian elements. Like all Victo-

ria's castles, the interior is equally impressive.

Inside the castle is a large hallway, decorated with Italian Carrara marble, silk panelled walls and a coffered-beam ceiling. In addition, a Palladian window filters light onto the staircase that leads upstairs. The rooms are decorated in marble, and antique chandeliers hang from the ceilings, although many of the original furnishings have long since gone.

Despite many changes over the years, it is still possible for the visitor to imagine what it must have been like to wander through the grounds of the castle in its early days. Today, the visitor approaches Spencer Castle from Topaz Avenue, off Cook Street. A picturesque garden reminiscent of a bailey circles the residence, and there is even a pond on the south side that reminds one of a miniature moat. When Spencer Castle was finished in 1914 it was considered one of the ten finest homes in Victoria.

Unfortunately, Griffith did not enjoy his opulent residence for very long. A dramatic slump in the building industry during World War One forced the architect to eventually sell his home; in 1918 it was purchased by David Scott Spencer, the son of Mr. David Spencer, one of Victoria's preeminent retail magnates. By then his father was living in the same mansion on Moss Street that had once served as the temporary residence of British Columbia's Lieutenant Governor after the disastrous fire at Cary Castle in 1899. Ironically, it was Spencer's Store which had supplied Samuel Maclure with the imported furnishings that were needed for the interior decoration of Government House. Nowadays the residence on Moss Street serves as the home of the Victoria Art

Gallery.

Spencer's Store was a fixture in Victoria's urban landscape for many years. Its founder, Mr. David Spencer, was born in Wales in 1837. He was a pioneer in the true sense of the word: Mr. Spencer sailed from Liver-

Spencer's Department Store, Victoria
BCA: E-09094

pool in 1862, reaching San Francisco via the Panama Canal; he then took a train for the final leg of the journey to Seattle, before settling in Victoria. He had originally intended to live in the interior, but he bought a bookstore in Victoria instead. A deeply religious man, Mr. Spencer ensured that all his business dealings were scrupulously honest, and by 1873 had formed a partnership in the city with Mr. Denny called 'Denny and Spencer'. A decade later he opened his own store on Government Street. Mr. Spencer's vision was to oper-

ate a retail store that focussed on volume, ensuring con-
sumers a wide selection at an affordable price — without sacrificing quality. At the turn of the 20th century,
Spencer's Store was selling everything from shoes and
clothing to furniture, china and kitchenware. By then
the store had become a forerunner of the modern department store. Unfortunately, tragedy struck one night
when Mr. Spencer least expected it.

In 1910 the store was burnt to the ground. The
business was rebuilt, however, and soon a chain of

Spencer family portrait (Middle: Mr. Spencer seated second from left; Mrs.
Spencer fourth from left; David Scott Spencer standing fourth from left)
BCA: H-01662

stores stretched across Vancouver Island and the Lower
Mainland, beckoning the customer with greater variety than ever before. As the business prospered, Mr.

Spencer continued to be active in the church, and gave generously to charity, founding an orphanage with the help of his devoted wife, who was also active in the temperance movement. The aging retail magnate lived

A view of Spencer Castle from the south lawn
AUTHOR

to be 83, finally dying at his home on Moss Street in 1920. The octogenarian was survived by his wife and 13 children — five of them boys.

David Scott Spencer, one of his five sons, bought the castle off Henry Sandham Griffith shortly before his father's death, and it soon became known as 'Spencer Castle'. 'Mr. Dave', as he was affectionately known by all, was a director of the company, and he is remembered by friends and associates alike as a "rollicking genial soul." As an heir to the Spencer empire, he continued the grand tradition started by his father, and never lost sight of his responsibilities both to the community and to his own employees, who enjoyed some unusually generous company benefits. David's brother, Chris, exemplified the family's spirit when he once told an audience: "If you want to be happy, don't pursue happiness as a goal. Just work hard, think of others as well as yourself, and be human."

By the end of World War Two, the Spencer family had nine stores, and over a thousand employees on the payroll. However, in 75 years of business the world had seen many changes, and the global economy was

Spencer Castle from the east lawn
AUTHOR

transforming itself yet again. Spencer's was now facing an uncertain future. It was Chris Spencer who finally had the unpleasant duty of addressing the employees in Vancouver in 1948: due to an insidious combination of ever increasing taxes, succession duties and stiff competition, it was impossible for an independent retail chain to survive in Canada. Sadly, a family store that had been part of British Columbia for nearly a century was taken over by the T. Eaton Company of Toronto. The board of directors was dissolved, and David retired to enjoy his golden years at Spencer Castle.

David and Kate lived at the castle for nearly two more decades. The Spencers adored their home, and decorated it with furniture, art and antiques from around the world. In the 1960s, the castle even won an award for the most outstanding alpine garden in North America. But as time marched on, David passed away and Kate eventually moved into an apartment; in 1963, the castle was converted into a museum. It wasn't long before there was pressure to develop the land. However, unlike Ashnola Castle, which was destroyed by the wrecking ball, steps were taken to preserve Spencer Castle: a condominium complex was erected nearby, and today the castle serves as a community centre for its residents. Henry Sandham Griffith would be pleased to know that the castle once considered one of the ten finest homes in Victoria still stands proudly today above the city at the top of Topaz Avenue. So too would the Spencer family, who exemplify the dedicated spirit that helped to build the city, earning the respect of their employees by using a management style that was quite different from that of the Dunsmuirs.

DIRECTIONS: *From downtown go north on Government Street; turn right on to Hillside; and then left on to Cook Street. 300 metres later make a left turn up a steep hill called The*

Rise — then turn right on to Topaz and you are there. Walking not recommended. It is a 15 minute ride from the Inner Harbour.

Conclusion

OUR STORY OF VICTORIA'S CASTLES has come to a close, and we have finally reached the end of our brief history of lovers, madmen, millionaires and ghosts on Canada's imperial margins. In many ways it is an astonishing story. Our journey has carefully examined Victoria's castles from several perspectives: we have explored their elegant exteriors, wandered through their lavish interiors, and we have taken a close look at the extraordinary people who lived in them. In retrospect, Victoria's castles are not real castles at all, but 'mock castles', 'follies' or 'neocastles', each representing a remarkable architectural achievement that is the product of powerful forces which helped to shape the Canadian landscape in the latter half of the 19th century.

One of the primary forces that triggered the castle craze in Victoria was money; obviously, all of these elegant homes testify to the personal wealth of the men who built them. In this sense they are symbols of the power of those who once lived here. Yet, despite their obvious wealth, a remarkable number of these men felt obligated to play a public role in their community; some may have been motivated by power, but others appear to have been impelled by a deep sense of noblesse oblige. It is an idea quite foreign to many people today, who embrace mass consumerism as an end in itself. For many of those who lived in these castles, therefore, wealth was an opportunity to serve the community. That being said, I suspect that very few of the men who built these elegant homes would have openly embraced the modern welfare state—philanthropy clearly had its limits.

It is hardly surprising that some of Victoria's castles reflect a Scottish ethnicity. Many of Victoria's early residents came from Scotland to work for the Hudson's Bay Company. Robert Dunsmuir, for example, was proud of his origins, even if he did advocate closer ties with the United States. Nevertheless, the most dominant style of castle in Victoria is not Scottish, but Anglo-Norman, although a trace of the chateauesque is evident in Craigdarroch Castle, the latter constructed partly through the prism of its American architect. What is clear is that some of these men did feel a need to distance themselves from their humble beginnings. However, the importance of Gothic Revivalism in Canada in the 19th century should not be underestimated. In retrospect, many of Victoria's early citizens may have been motivated to replicate these ideas precisely because of their exposure to a wilderness that was so alien to them. Yet in the end perhaps the only dominant characteristic of Victoria's castles is their high degree of eclecticism. Given the astonishing variety of characters who built them, perhaps this is not surprising—and the city is all the richer because of it.

It is important to note the role technology played in the development of Victoria's castles. Not only did the advent of the railway permit greater flexibility in the choice of building materials for the construction of castles, but some residents were able to invest even greater profits into the construction of their residences as the city became more fully integrated into the modern industrial-capitalist economy. Craigdarroch Castle, for example, shows evidence of the former, and Hatley Castle proudly attests to the latter. It goes without saying, of course, that there never really was a serious attempt to replicate a landed aristocracy in western Canada. The type of economy that made castles possible in Victoria was characterised by upward mobility, not rigid class distinctions. Moreover, partible inheritance (leaving an estate to all the children in a family) was favoured over primogeniture (leaving land to the firstborn), and this further undermined the establishment of a hereditary aristocracy. It also partly explains why none of the castles built in Victoria serve as residences today. Nevertheless, Victoria's castles have proven to be extremely resilient artifices in the city, adapting themselves over the years to a remarkably wide range of functions. Given the unique characteristics of these buildings, there is no reason to suppose that they will not continue to be useful artifices in the future.

Spencer Castle was the last grand home to be built in Victoria with a martial facade, but it was not the end of the castle. The iconography of the castle continued to be replicated in the urban landscape throughout the

20th century. In 1915, for example, the architect Colonel Ridgway Wilson built the Bay Street Armoury in the form of an Anglo-Norman castle; two years later he designed the Wilkinson Road Prison by incorporating a similar facade. City merchants have continued to popularise the theme in buildings such as the Tudor Pub in Esquimalt, the Oxford Castle Inn along Gorge Road, and the Castle Pub in Sooke. Castles — particularly the Bavarian style found in Disney World — now appear regularly on miniature golf courses throughout British Columbia, and advertisements in Victoria make extensive use of this iconography on their logos. So, what does it all mean?

Well, the forces that inspire merchants to employ castle motifs today are rather different from those that inspired Victoria's wealthiest citizens a century ago, just as the forces that created these 'neocastles' were very different from those that prompted the erection of castles in the Middle Ages. Security, durability, quality, and prestige are all words that we have now come to associate with castles, which partly explains why they are such useful icons in the advertising business. But nearly all of those who reflect upon castles today share one more sentiment in common — a romantic attachment to the past. It's easy to overlook the exclusivity of the castle, because castles evoke scenes of knights in shining armour, minstrels, and pretty maidens, ideas that prove just as appealing to us today as they did to Don Quixote, who would no doubt be equally eager to joust at skyscrapers as he was to joust at windmills. But in the end, perhaps what we see in the castle is the fulfilment of a deep longing that resides in all of us — besides, who wouldn't want to live in a castle?

GLOSSARY

Bailey	Courtyard (see Ward)
Barbican	Outward extension of a gate
Battlement	Crenellation (q.v.)
Bay Window	Lower protruding window
Chateau	Fortified French mansion
Chemin de Ronde	Walkway around a tall tower
Coping	Protective upper covering for a wall
Corbel	Projection from a wall, intended to support a weight
Crenellation	Opening in the upper portion of a wall (see Battlement, Merlon and Embrasure)
Dormer	A projection from a pitched roof forming a structure of its own
Drawbridge	Bridge that can be raised or lowered, usually across a Moat (q.v.)
Embrasure	Splayed opening in a wall for a window (see Merlon)
Fenestration	Arrangement of windows in a building
Finial	Ornament on top of a pinnacle
Gable	Triangular upper portion of a wall abutting steep overhanging roof
Great Tower	Keep, usually stone
Hall	Principal room in a medieval house

Keep   Great Tower (q.v.)

Loggia   Gallery adjoining a building that is
                   open on one side and supported by
                   pillars

Loop   Arrow slit (often decorative)

Merlon   Vertical parapet in a wall between
                   Embrasures (q.v.)

Motte   Artificial mound of earth on which a
                   castle sits

Moat   Water in the ditch surrounding a
                   castle

Mullion   Upright, separating the glass in a
                   divided window

Oriel   Protruding upper window

Porte-Cochère Literally, 'doorway for a coach'; stone
                   shelter protecting the main entrance
                   to a residence (see Barbican)

Quoined   Term used to describe the corners of
                   a building when embellished with
                   dressed stone

Sill   Slab at the foot of a window

Solar   Room adjacent to a hall (often
                   exposed to sunlight)

Ward   Courtyard (see Bailey)

SELECT BIBLIOGRAPHY

Bingham, J. *Samuel Maclure Architect.* Horsdal and Schubert. Ganges, B.C.: 1985

Castle, G. and B.F. King. *Victoria Landmarks.* G. Castle. Victoria:1985

Castle, G. and B.F. King. *More Victoria Landmarks.* Sono Nis Press. Victoria: 1988

Castle, G., ed. *Hatley Park: An Illustrated Anthology.* The Friends of Hatley Park Society. Hatley Park, B.C.: 1995

Cotton, P. *Vice-Regal Mansions of British Columbia.* Elgin Publications. Victoria: 1981

Jackman, S.W. *The Men at Cary.* Morriss. Victoria: 1972

Kalman, H.D. *A History of Canadian Architecture.* Oxford University Press. Toronto: 2000

Luxton, D. *Builders of the West: The Early Architects of British Columbia.* Talon. Vancouver: 2003

Reksten, T. *Rattenbury.* Sono Nis Press. Victoria: 1978

Reksten, T. *Craigdarroch: The Story of Dunsmuir Castle.* Orca Book Publishers. Victoria: 1987

Reksten, T. *The Dunsmuir Saga.* Douglas and McIntyre, Toronto: 1991

Segger, M. *Victoria: A Primer for Regional History in Architecture.* Milestone Publications. Victoria: 1979

Segger, M. *The Buildings of Samuel Maclure.* Sono Nis Press. Victoria: 1986

Segger, M. and D. Franklin. *Exploring Victoria's Architecture.* Sono Nis Press. Victoria: 1996

Ward, R. *Echoes of Empire: Victoria and its Remarkable Buildings.* Harbour Pub. Madeira Park, B.C.: 1996

INDEX

Hollywood 95, 98
Hopkins, Mark 30
Hopper, Edna Wallace 41
Hudson's Bay Company 1, 15, 27, 114
Hughes, Griffith R. 42

I

Illegitimate offspring 98
Industrial Revolution 3
Isle of Skye 15, 17
Italian Renaissance style 30
Italianate 29
Italianate garden 87

J

Jackman, Sydney 42
James, Percy Leonard 78
Japanese garden 87

K

Kaiser Wilhelm 90
Kennedy, Arthur (Gov.) 9
Kew Gardens 87
Kiel Ship Canal 89
Kilmarnock 26
King George VI 97
Kipling, Rudyard 71
Kishita, Isaburo 87

L

Lady Dufferin 11
Lady in White 99
Laurier, Wilfrid (Prime Minister) 66